the Winter GARDENER

A Woman's Journey from Futile to Fertile

the Winter GARDENER

A Woman's Journey from Futile to Fertile

Patricia Hetherington

Patricia Hetherington

Rose Pointe Publishing

Gibsons, British Columbia

Library and Archives Canada Cataloguing in Publication

Hetherington, Patricia, 1948-
The winter gardener : a woman's journey from futile to fertile / Patricia Hetherington.

Includes index.
ISBN 978-0-9782795-0-9

1. Hetherington, Patricia, 1948-. 2. Self-actualization (Psychology)
3. Spiritual biography--Canada. I. Title.

BF637.S4H489 2007 *204.092*
C2007-900377-X

Rose Pointe Publishing
1382 Burns Road
Gibsons, British Columbia
Canada V0N 1V1
604 886 9559
www.thewintergardener.ca

Text design and photography
Arlene Littler © 2007

Printed in Canada

For my daughter Sarah

The garden must be prepared
in the soul first, or else it will not flourish.

Hebrew Proverb

TABLE OF CONTENTS

PROLOGUE

Crucifixion by Water

In my dream I must endure a crucifixion by water. Although desperately afraid, I throw myself into the circular pool that has been prepared for this purpose. I am held suspended in the water by a neck clamp that forces me to wait and watch, in horror, as the waters rise slowly towards my throat. It is inevitable that I will drown.

A male informant conveys silently to me that while I cannot avoid this ritual, there is a remote possibility that I will survive the process. Regardless of the outcome, I must surrender.

YEAR ONE

October 31, 1996 **Gibsons, British Columbia**

hob•ble \ˈhä-bəl *vb* to fasten together the legs of a horse to prevent straying; to move along unsteadily or with difficulty.

I slam the red lacquer door behind Sarah and her father, Brian, who has come to take her out for Halloween trick-or-treating. A strange brew of loss and bitterness boils inside me. *Why am I left alone with Nala, the marmalade cat, doing the dutiful thing, holding down the home and handing out candy, while they go out together?*

I picture my seven-year-old daughter disappearing down the driveway, her black witch's cape billowing out behind her, and wonder about my own choice of clothing: leggings, fleece shirt and socks. *Why am I not dressed in something that matches tonight's ominous mood?* Unlike the silky costumes that I've gravitated to in past years, I should be pulling on a hideous mask or draping my tall body in the black shrouds of death and mourning.

I move towards the cassette recorder on the hutch and press the Play button. *Sounds of Horror* fill the room. The din foments my foreboding. Turning around, I give the emaciated vinyl skeleton that Sarah has hung from the downstairs light fixture a good swift whack and head back upstairs to sit in the garden room.

Knowing what I'm planning to do tonight, I rein in my

thoughts to keep them from running away on me. Nala joins me briefly on the sofa until the door bell jolts us rudely. The sound of children's voices calling out downstairs forces us to respond. The cat is thrown into a perplexed heap on the floor as I stand up to greet the insistent callers. After two or three such interruptions, Nala gives up in disgust and wanders off to lie on my bed.

By 5:30 they're home again. Sarah announces, "It's too early," which means, *No one's out yet and it's still not scary enough.*

Besides, they're hungry now and ready for Hamburger Soup, which has become our family's favourite for Halloween supper. Father and daughter inhale the soup with only minor damage sustained to Sarah's green painted face from the occasional splash of broth. Well fed and proud of the pile of candy they've dumped on the kitchen floor, they embark boisterously on the second round of door-knocking. For me, time stretches unbearably.

8:00. They burst through the door, Sarah triumphant with her riches of Skittles, Smarties, Glosette Peanuts and Raisins, Reese's Pieces, Snickers, Aeros, Chiclets and popcorn balls. I'm caught between conflicting values: wanting to match her enthusiasm over what she calls her "loot" and, at the same time, hating the sight of these goodies, knowing that each one is loaded with additives and devoid of food value. One item in particular becomes the focus of my ire. I hold up a roll of pastel tablets called Tingles and demand haughtily, "What are these?" I spit out my words, "I swear they're vinyl."

Sarah chooses to ignore my remark but my sudden nastiness cuts through the pretence that this is a happily functioning family.

The excitement of the night finally catches up to Brian who's exhausted from his efforts to keep pace with his daughter running up and down the hills in the neighbourhood. Declaring, "I've had it," he notifies us that he intends to leave for his home.

"Would you give me a hand with Sarah before you go?" I ask.

"Sure," he replies, picking her up and plunking her down on the washing machine next to the laundry sink. I wipe off the remains of her face paint and she is on her way to bed.

I catch Brian as he's making a quick retreat. "I'd like to talk to you later," I say, looking at this man who has been my husband for ten years.

He replies easily, "Give me a call," and then he's gone.

As I close the door, I realize that I've forced my hand with these innocent-sounding words. I am now committed to my course of action.

9:10. I tiptoe into Sarah's room to make sure she's sound asleep before undertaking the challenge that awaits me. She's purring, quiet as a kitten, and I know that if I delay any longer, Brian will also be asleep. I pick up the cordless phone and return to the garden room, which is now considerably colder than when I settled in with Nala a couple of hours earlier. I stretch out on the same sofa and dial his number. *It's now or never.*

The phone rings. I hear him pick up the receiver, identify himself in his customary way.

An imperial moment opens before me, compelling me to be fully present, compelling me to mark the occasion, after which the lives of three people will be irrevocably altered.

"Hi, Brian, it's me." I move into the moment.

Time does not exist. I pause for what may be six seconds or an hour, resisting the temptation to reiterate what he already knows. *You've been living with Mary for over two years now, ever since we've been separated.* I resist the temptation to muddy the message with too many words. *And even though you've found a new relationship, it seems I can't, not while I'm still married to you. In fact, a friend recently remarked that she thought of you as having two wives.* I resist the temptation to dilute the impact of my words. *I suppose it's no accident that I haven't met anyone these past two years whom I've been remotely interested in. Maybe that's because I've made myself impervious to my longing, living like a maiden aunt in my big house—noble, beyond reproach.* I resist the temptation to prolong the pain of ambiguity any longer. *Even though Sarah seems content enough with our arrangement, I worry that she's getting some strange ideas about marriage and relationships.* I resist the temptation to confound my courage, reminding myself, *God, Patricia, this is not a life; this is not good enough! You've been living in limbo.*

Pare down. Pare down. Cut to the quick. Be decisive.

"I can't do this anymore. I want a divorce."

I expect him to lash out with righteous anger, accuse me of betrayal, or blame me for messing up Sarah's childhood. Instead he responds, not with his ample energy, but with quiet agreement, "I suppose you're right. Neither of us seems to be making any move towards reconciliation. I'll contact a lawyer to draw up the papers when I return from Sweden next month."

Maybe now, five years to the day that we arrived on the Sunshine Coast, and tonight—on Halloween—we can finally take off our masks and stop pretending.

November 2, 1996 **Gibsons, British Columbia**

wres•tle \'re-səl\ *vb* to engage in deep thought, consideration or debate; to engage in, or as if in, a violent or determined struggle.

How I detest this time and place I find myself in. One minute I'm full of optimism. Take this morning, for instance. When I awaken, even before I open my eyes, I'm humming a curious tune. *"Ooh, I want to dance with somebody, I want to feel the heat with somebody … somebody to love."* The next minute I want to murder. The constriction of my world feels like a straightjacket squeezing the life out of me. I am either cowed and humbled in the face of my life pressing down on me or swamped by a surfeit of emotion and the need to scrutinize every thought, dream, or barely-felt feeling. Driven by this hyper awareness, I'm constantly asking, *Does this word, this gesture, this event, or this dream have meaning, and if so, what?*

Then again, at times I manage to connect with an essential part of myself and function with confidence, humour, and occasionally, wisdom. An uneasy peace at best. I never know when a ferocious front will move in and stop me dead in my tracks. Never know when I'll feel the warmth of hope again. I am constantly buffeted, always in reaction, with no solid ground upon which to stand.

Still, I know that this passage requires that I drown in the unknowing, with no guarantee as to how, or whether, I will emerge once this primal storm has passed. The dark goddess drags me to the water's edge by my hair, forcing me down on my knees, demanding that I bow to her immutable power and finally admit to my own utter despair and powerlessness.

At the age of forty-eight, my life is levelled to one daughter, one cat, one sister, Joann, a new degree and a partially-finished work of embroidery. I no longer have a husband and my future is uncertain. While I believed that I had picked up the mantle of a more noble profession when I completed a master's degree in counselling, I suffer the indignity of what feels like a regressive move, accepting a part time job in the sales office of a waterfront condominium project.

After Sarah leaves for school, I pick up my embroidery, which has had me stumped since I laid it down two days ago. I can see the problem, but not what to do about it. And while I know that the solution will appear in its own time, what I need to do now is get out of my own way long enough for that to happen. But waiting for solutions to surface—either in embroidery or life—is more difficult than it sounds.

I think back to a tape I listened to recently called *The Creative Fire* by Clarissa Pinkola Estés. She reminds me that when a project bogs down, we must stop. *Cut back. Tear away.* I understand her logic, yet this seemingly paradoxical advice irritates me. As usual, I would rather do *more* than less. In this case, adding one needless stitch after another to an already overworked area.

After this two-day hiatus and coming back to my embroidery with fresh eyes, I suddenly see what I need to do. As she suggests, I begin to snip and pull out a series of tiny coloured threads. *One step forward, two steps back.* The energy finally unblocked, I'm moving forward again. A lesson in life.

My challenge is to rid myself of the mistaken belief that *any action* is better than *no action*, or the convoluted logic that tricks me into believing that *going anywhere* is better than *going nowhere.* I must start to distinguish between genuine movement and empty motions, which are useless except for the temporary salve they apply to the anxiety that claws incessantly at my brain. The questions I ask myself constantly reveal my self-contempt. *Writing a journal and embroidering ... you call that a life?* Or the despair, *Is this all there is? Dear God, tell me it isn't so.*

I think back to my Athena self, the warrior goddess and archetype of clear-headed action in Greek mythology who ran my life in my 20's and 30's. These days, Athena is disgusted about most things in my life: the home in a rural setting that denies me the opportunity to associate, or compete, with powerful men; the lack of purposeful employment in which I produce enviable results such as those in my commercial real estate career in the 1980's; the midlife career change to counselling, which is governed less by strategy and will than by intuition and introspection; the unwillingness or inability to continue dressing in the warrior's dazzling armour that would keep me emotionally aloof. Athena cringes to behold what feels like my fall from grace, marked by the death of certainty, the dawning of dissonance. Outwardly, she rails. Inwardly, she grieves the loss of this impressive self.

I am making my way across a landscape that I have never before encountered. At times it is only my words and the spider-silk tethers that trail out behind each word like a safety cord that keep me from slipping away completely.

Why do I write? I write because of a promise to myself that I will journal for one year, thereby imposing structure and meaning onto a life where none exists. I write because speaking of my terror keeps me from being destroyed by it.

Speaking of terror, I begin asking questions similar to those which Deena Metzger, poet, author and cancer survivor, poses in *The Book of Hags. Why are so many women in their 40's and 50's getting this particular disease at this particular time?* Does it have to do with silence, which she postulates is the root of cancer? When we cannot express what needs to be said, do our words erupt in the only way available to us: in the form of a raging growth? This causes me to wonder, *Does unexpressed terror, buried in our bodies, become cancer? The terror of stinking clots of words and maggoty emotions that turns against us and eats our own flesh? Is cancer a form of terror made manifest as disease?*

Is this the same terror that tells me I'll never find another husband, lover or partner? That tells me I'll never find my place in the world, a career which allows me to serve, or an authentically creative life? Terror that tells me that my own cold hands are the only hands that will touch my body?

When I see women who are roughly the same age as I am, I look closely for clues that reveal how they're holding up to this question of terror. I know what to look for—tension, brittleness, eyes that remain lifeless when they smile—evidence of suppressed feeling and an attempt to conceal the truth. Knowing these are my alternatives, I choose to release this terror from my body by writing about it instead.

This last thought evokes a sudden surge of energy. I pick up my embroidery again and study the area I've just re-worked. *It's still not right.* I rip it out again; start over again. Forced to concede for the second time today that I can't push the river.

Suddenly I'm sick to death of all of this: the tedious work, the struggle to find meaning, the metaphors. I toss the offending bundle of hoop, fabric, thread and needles onto a nearby chair and walk away. I pose one final question that Deena might ask. *Why do I choose this particular kind of writing at this particular time?*

Because, I reply, calling upon myself to cut through the abstractions, *I know that I can write a complete sentence. What I don't know is whether I can tell the truth.*

November 5, 1996 **Gibsons, British Columbia**

ache \'āk *vb* to suffer a dull persistent pain; to become distressed as with anxiety, regret or yearning.

Two things happen around the same time. I declare that I want a divorce and I receive a call from John, a man I met in Vancouver at a professional training, saying that he might visit this weekend. Coming together, these events compound and unleash a sexual imperative to *get going again*. Suddenly energies contained within the crushingly narrow roles I inhabit as friend, sister, mother, counsellor and teacher demand fuller expression. And with the possible presence of a man, it is now safe to admit to my own raw readiness that I have denied for fear of going completely mad. Hearing this news, my sensuous self, long under lock and key, snaps to attention; serves notice that she is returning. A date has been set for my likely release from solitary confinement and Pandora's box of sexual longing is opened. The woman who emerges is bold and clear.

I spent most of yesterday performing rituals that I imagine are those same rituals that women throughout time have performed in anticipation of being with a man. I have my legs waxed, my hair trimmed, sit long enough for a manicure and pedicure to dry, and finally, purchase a small bottle of patchouli and ylang ylang massage oil. The sense of well-being awakened by yesterday's pampering lingers as I lie in bed this morning. At the same time, I am aware that I should get Sarah off to school.

Our morning routine is smooth and uneventful: breakfast, dressing, teeth, books, bag ... a good-bye kiss. I lock the door behind her, turn quickly towards the stairs and leap them two at a time, moving towards the garden room, the sofa, and my pleasure. For a few moments, I manage to push aside my frantic drive to figure out where the hell I'm going in my life. In anticipation of sexual pleasure, if only temporary, I allow the morning to become still, unhurried. I stretch out on the sofa, wiggle my body into the plush pillows to find the optimum position, and settle down like a contented cat purring and preening herself.

Erica Jong's deliciously wicked book, *The Fear of Flying*, pops into my mind. Following merrily along her line of thinking, I reason, *Even though I may be flying in tandem soon, there's still no reason why I can't fly solo right now!*

Despite the chill of the November morning, the east-facing atrium is already quite warm. For a second I entertain the absurd notion that my Italian neighbour, wanting to talk about harvesting my kiwi fruit and whistling *O Solo Mio,* will wander up to my top deck, peer through the window, and catch me *in the act.* But laughing at the sheer nonsense of this thought, I discount the idea and dispense with any hesitation.

Becoming my own lover, I slip my hands under my cotton T-shirt and run them over my small breasts, caressing them in rounded motions. I tweak my nipples to tautness, slide my hands over the flatness of my belly and across my hips in wide, generous strokes, and over the mound of my pubis. My body relaxes and opens. I touch my own wetness.

Sufficiently aroused, I reach down to pull off my green lycra leggings and underwear and throw them onto the floor. Lying spread-eagled, naked from the waist down, left leg tossed over a back cushion and right leg angled towards the floor, I position myself to feel the warmth of the morning sun push gently against my body. Slowly, I begin to rub my clitoris, whispering my own sweet profanities as if uttered by a man ... when Nala takes a sudden flying leap and lands squarely on my chest.

From her vantage point she gazes solemnly down on me, her tiny face only inches from my own, her breath soft on my skin. Caught off guard by this unexpected visit from my feline friend, I muse, *What do I do now? Do I ignore her and carry on?* But the magic of my self-ministrations is broken. The cat's curiosity does little to serve the sensuality of the moment and I quickly conclude that I cannot continue in this compromised position.

Grasping the indignant creature firmly around the mid-section with both hands, I sweep her off my chest and heave her unceremoniously onto the floor, satisfied that I am finished with her. Yet Nala has presented me with another conundrum. Now that I've touched her, do I continue to touch myself, with cat hands? Or do I wander into the kitchen like a lady centaur, clothed on top, naked on bottom, wash my hands, and start over?

That's precisely what I do, urging myself at last to a well-deserved climax and muttering, *To hell with Nala, to hell with everyone!*

Already, I feel much better.

November 12, 1996 **Gibsons, British Columbia**

re•store **\re'stōr** *vb* to bring back or put into a former or original state; to repair; re-establish, renew.

John didn't visit after all, calling Friday instead to say, "Somethings come up ... sorry, I can't make it ... maybe later in the month." My initial response is off-handed: nothing ventured, nothing gained. But upon exploring deeper and recalling the perfunctory way he addresses me, I discover feelings of anger and below that, a residue of shame.

There's something else this morning as well. Feelings of vulnerability—not the existential variety—but the cosmetic variety, which arise simultaneously with an appointment at the hairdresser's for colouring.

Sitting over breakfast, chewing thoughtfully on my homemade granola, I find myself thinking about the issue of power, a curious thing particularly as it relates to none other than my hairdresser whose power over me is legion. Greater by far than the other women to whom I entrust the private aspects of my personal care: wax lady, accountant, reflexologist. My hairdresser stands in a league all her own, her power commensurate with her singular ability to reduce me to spasms of humiliation or lift me, body, mind and spirit, to new heights of possibility. Hers is nothing short of the power to transform consciousness. Nothing to be snivelled at!

What has brought me to this moment of reckoning is a woman's way of knowing that the time has come to undergo a familiar, but daunting, cosmetic rite of passage. The knowledge becomes progressively more alarming when I look at myself in the mirror these days. Instead of seeing my own face, I see the face of my mother on the black and white television screen in a hospital morgue. Twenty hours after her untimely death, her features had already twisted strangely out of shape. Studying my own face this morning, I recognize the November pallor of my skin (dull and drab against my hair) and realize that there is nothing I can do to remove this inevitable cup from myself.

I drive to my appointment, see myself in, and stake claim to the only chair not covered with unfolded laundry, newspapers, mail or animals. I reach down to pick up an old copy of *Maclean's, Canada's Weekly News magazine* lying on the coffee table and behold Hillary Clinton in coiffed composure on the cover, her arm draped proprietarily around the shoulder of her president husband, Bill Clinton.

This synchronistic discovery pleases me immensely, adding fuel to my musings about power, presentation and beauty. Blonde and polished, she smiles easily at me. I wonder, *Does her position of power make her any less anxious in the face of this odious initiation? How does she react when confronted with a bottle of peroxide, or by a reflection of herself in the mirror with a cap tied under her chin, her hair poking out of the plastic pores in a frizzy aureole—like green alfalfa sprouts in a styrofoam container?*

Not well, I venture to guess, despite her considerable presence on the world stage. Probably not much better than I do, sitting here in the spare-bedroom salon of my hairdresser where I'm feeling only slightly mollified by the busy chatter of what I count as eight assorted birds in two large wicker cages. *When did she get those things?*

"What are they?" I wonder aloud.

"Oh," she replies, cooing and cuddling a dusty-orange bird up to her face, "this is a peach-faced lovebird. The others are Indonesian ring-neck parakeets and zebra finches."

Despite her affection for her feathered friends, I notice myself withholding admiration, having caught the cheeky little devils flinging not only bits of seeds and shells from their breakfast bowl, but also the occasional bit of bird dropping out of their cages and onto the floor next to me.

My hairdresser applies a frothy mixture onto the skinny strands of hair sticking out of the cap and rubs my skull vigorously, working the product into my hair. Next, she ushers me into the converted laundry room, points to a chair in front of the sink, waits for me to sit down, and finally cranks my head backwards over the sink.

"Now just relax," she announces emphatically. With that, she flicks off the light.

"Put your feet up on the wall," she calls from another room, "it'll take the pressure off your neck."

I do as I'm told. She's right. I do feel more comfortable, although not any happier. I need my writing materials.

"Can you bring me my pencil and paper?" I call out from the darkened room. If nothing else, I can capture my feelings of dread as I sit-out the allotted time, pencil and paper in my lap and my feet on the wall in front of me.

Trapped in the tiny room like a prisoner, my awareness sharpens suddenly. I examine every sound and smell in the house, wondering, *How will this impact the outcome of my hair?* I'm suspicious of any omen that may stack the deck against me:

the twittering of birds in the room down the hall, the whirring of clothes in the dryer next to me, the muffled sounds of *Another World* coming from the television set in the living room. *Will she become so engrossed in the program that she will forget about me? Will she leave on the solution too long and fry my hair?* Other matters, like the cigarette smoke that I detect the moment I open the front door, alarm me as well. *Will the frothy chemicals on my hair react with the smoke and turn my hair bright yellow or orange?*

With my fears rushing wildly over me, I realize that only by putting pencil to paper will I regain the slightest sense of control over what's happening to me and thereby prevent a total emotional wash-out. Arming myself with these modest supplies, I now possess the power to create my own response to this alarming situation, if only by virtue of the fact that I can choose to employ a tongue-in-cheek tone as a strategy to dilute my feelings of foreboding.

The cap is coming off! *Dear God, may it not be brassy-gold! May it be Hillary-blonde and nothing short of glorious!* I turn to my hairdresser in this pregnant moment, waiting for her verdict from on high.

Finally, she delivers the ultimate proclamation, "Much better!" Suddenly, all is well with my world.

I feel the tension, which has corseted my body like the black vinyl cape wrapped around my shoulders and torso, slide off in a single fluid motion. My hairdresser and I share a magnificent moment! I relax luxuriously, inhale and exhale with loud satisfaction, utter a low audible groan of relief, and allow her her delighted ministrations. She purrs over me not unlike the way she fusses over her birds.

Quick to grab our pleasure as it appears, we grant

ourselves the gift of giddiness now that the tension of the perilous ritual has lifted. Our buoyant mood is heightened to a mildly manic pitch by the sobering knowledge that things could have turned out very differently.

Could have had us scrambling madly to gather our wits together as we tried to figure out what the hell to do next. Could have had us despairing at the idea of spending the next three hours locked together in resentful communion, trying to undo the mess—she biting back her desire to complain about the crummy hand she'd been dealt and me, sullen and gravely distressed, struggling not to let her know how resentful I am of the power she wields over me. More than ever, I would be dependant upon her whims and humour, good or otherwise. This sort of scene can get very ugly. Such is the stay of execution that we have been handed by the gods. Yes, you bet we're giddy!

The moment of terror has ended; the spectre of the angel of hideous hair leaving her mark on my door, has passed. I make my evaluation at my leisure.

"This," I pronounce grandly, the stress of the whole experience culminating in sudden hyperbole, "may be the finest hair colouring I've ever had!"

Shortly thereafter, I pick up a mirror to look at the back of my head. Even as I notice the small spikes of bleached hair which I usually detest, I quickly classify this effect as a minor irritant and retain my magnanimous mood. Besides, my hair looks great from the front, which is what's most important. Now that I'm more blonde than dark, it's safe to wear black this holiday season without running the risk that another First Nations teenage boy, like the one I encountered in a grade nine class during my counselling internship, would ask, "Doesn't she look like Cruella De Vil?"

Upon hearing this remark, my staggered ego rushed to defend itself with a marginally comforting thought. *There must be a cultural difference between what does, and doesn't, constitute beauty.*

The Path

In my dream I am shown "my path," which is not a path at all. There is nothing to indicate that a path exists. Every place I look is impassable and covered with thick brambles. I wonder who could possibly travel this route. Yet despite these obstacles, I am not fazed by what I see. I consider the path briefly and think calmly to myself, "I can do this."

November 14, 1996 **Gibsons, British Columbia**

stifle \'stī-fəl *vb* to suffocate, smother; to kill by depriving of oxygen; to withhold from circulation or expression.

Still lying in bed before I'm fully awake, I feel the dull band of a headache across my eyes. *I wonder what this headache is about?* Most likely it has to do with the interview I had yesterday with the director of human resources at the local pulp mill, ostensibly to discuss whether my skills might complement their corporate needs for counselling or training. I flashback to the meeting.

Leaning his body towards me from his chair he asks, "Now that you've finished your master's degree, what do you want to do?"

I struggle to contain the immediate feelings this question triggers, groping my way through a mental maze of confusion that suddenly threatens to pull me into a bottomless hole. Remembering to breathe, I try to answer his question as honestly as I can without betraying my increasing sense of panic.

Sitting in the chair opposite him, my leather skirt riding up on my thighs, I suddenly feel overdressed and ridiculous, my skirt too short and me too old, a fading Delta Dawn trying to look contemporary. Sick with horror and shame,

I'm already slipping away. I've lost the thread of connection to myself.

Athena's emotional armour that protected me well in the past, has worn thin as a result of my counselling training, making it increasingly unnatural not to disclose what I'm feeling. I want to be seen accurately. This is what drives me these days. Imposing constraints on our conversation as I find myself doing, I feel like a caricature of my former self, fraudulent and foolish.

Again, I face the issue of dissonance. Conflicting impulses clash below the surface of a commonplace conversation.

This is what I want to scream. This is what I stuff back into my throat. *I'm in shock because I realize that I'm not really employable; I value my independence and creative freedom too much for that. But that's not to say that coming to this realization has been an easy shift for me. It hasn't. I still feel the pain of giving up the illusion that there is a blueprint for my life, if only I could get my hands on it; a map that comforts me with its lack of ambiguity and points me directly towards the next phase in my life, personal and professional. I long for clean succinct words to describe who I am, what I'm doing.*

I do not tell him that I'm reeling from an essential reordering of my entire psyche, a sloughing off of one thing after another. *Dear God, when will it ever end?* I spare him talk about my marriage; my life as I imagined it would be; my husband's love, which provided a place to stand; the easy confidence of knowing that I was exactly where I wanted to be; the safety and status of being a wife.

My family, once the shape of a snug circle, is now gaping and lopsided. I bite back the desire to cite those items belonging to Brian that I still have to ferret out of my home: the suits hanging in the downstairs closet, the shoes

I used to polish, the ski clothes and equipment, the navy windsurfing towel (a gift from his first wife), which I still use in the laundry room for cleaning up after gardening or washing Sarah's hands.

I omit the word *hopeless*. Still, I need to speak about this pain, the sense that there is no meaning. *How can I sit here and talk about contracts when the golden souffle that I used to be is flat ... used up ... dead? When I feel more like scrambled eggs in a blender?*

How do I explain that for three months I've struggled to find the right words to put on a new business card? Tried to describe what it is that people should hire me to do? And at the same time, deal with the dashed expectation that I would finish university and emerge, fully formed like Athena, brilliant and dazzling, launching myself immediately into an impressive career?

Moment by moment, I must learn to live in the tension between what *has been* and what *will be*, and try not to go crazy in the process. My only consolation is believing that a new self will gradually appear and trusting that this nascent being will satisfy me more than the souffle I can no longer pretend to be. Ultimately, when I settle on words for my card, I go with action words that suggest the possibility of becoming something more: Counselling & Consulting. These words give me a sense of hope.

On this more upbeat note, I suddenly realize that I've had enough digging in this dreary emotional soil. I need a change of scenery and drive to my sister's home for a hot tub.

As I soak outside in the steaming water, looking out over the ocean, a light drizzle falls on my head. Seagulls perch on darkened logs. Their grey and white forms turn brilliant as the sun breaks through the clouds. Preening and visiting, they make little sound. A golden leaf from the plum tree drops into the water; it floats silently. Everything slows down.

I don't need to have the definitive word on myself today. I can give myself this day, this time in my life, to let it unfold.

This last thought brings unexpected tears to my eyes. The sudden gesture of charity I extend to myself allows me to admit that I'm exhausted from the effort of trying to figure it all out. No wonder my head hurts.

November 18, 1996 **Gibsons, British Columbia**

sa•vour **\'sā-vər** *vb* to season, give flavour to; to taste or smell with pleasure; to relish, delight in.

I awaken at the sound of my bedroom door opening. Sarah is standing there, fully dressed. *This is curious. What's she doing up so early?* She walks into the room, looks down on me still nestled in my bed, and launches into a complaint about Nala who spent the night on her bed—fidgeting—making it hard for her to sleep. Looking at the digital clock, I make a quick calculation. She's had ten hours of sleep. My mother's intuition for these things tells me that the cat is not the issue. Something else has prompted this sudden readiness for the day.

"Look," she announces importantly, clattering up the mini blinds of my bedroom window, "it's snowed again!" Because she bears this news, she claims proprietary credit for this marvel of nature.

In the luxury of this morning moment with my daughter, I allow her excitement to warm my feelings of well-being and climb out of bed to stand next to her. Sensory impressions surround us. Crisp white lace curtains frame the window and offer a view onto a world of white outside the room. The branches of the giant cedar trees droop under the weight of wet snow. The fig tree is covered with snow, creating a curious mix of Mediterranean and West Coast elements. The few remaining clusters of grapes not eaten by eager children or hungry birds, hang black and shrivelled after last night's frost. The sound of cars whizzing by on the highway is different. Muffled. Sloppy wet. Even the feeling-tone of the morning has changed. A blanket of contentment covers the room.

Now as excited as Sarah to begin the day, I announce, "This looks like a porridge sort of day to me," harkening back to the same logic I heard as a child.

'On cold mornings, you need hot cereal to stick to your ribs.'

Although I suspect that she doesn't like oatmeal any better than I liked the Red River Cereal that I was served on winter mornings in northern British Columbia, I'm still bent on making oatmeal for her.

She pays little attention to my words, secure in the knowledge that she, too, has power because of a long-standing agreement that if *I* get the satisfaction of feeding her a wholesome breakfast (either granola or cereal), then *she* gets to choose the toppings. In this case, a generous helping of brown sugar and cinnamon. Reading *The Paper Bag Princess* by Robert Munsch aloud to me, she eats her hearty breakfast with an exaggerated air of indifference. Clearly, we are both pleased with the start to the day. Now she wants me to walk her to school so that she can use her toboggan on the hill behind the playground.

When I hear her use the word *toboggan* I feel a sharp sudden ache. What she calls a toboggan is nothing more than a piece of heavy plastic with a hole cut at one end for a handle. I doubt that she's ever seen an old wooden toboggan. The kind with the rolled back front and long slats running lengthwise; with the shorter horizontal ribs running across to provide strength and stability, as well as a rough measurement of the space allotted for each child.

Sarah doesn't know that tobogganing isn't a solo sport or that the whole idea is about being together. Crouched and holding on for dear life to the person in front of you—careening out of control down a hill—and landing in a heap of bodies at the bottom. She doesn't know that a plastic toboggan is a travesty.

Suddenly I'm thinking, *If I can ignore the fact that she's already asked for a Playmobile doll house and blue sparkling nail polish in her early October letter to Santa, maybe I can give her something handcrafted instead. Like one of the beautiful wooden doll cradles that I saw a man selling in the mall last Christmas.* I latch onto this idea like a child clutching a toy, already anticipating the satisfaction.

As I return home after walking Sarah to school, my mind flits from one topic to another like a chickadee on a frozen feeder. I'm thinking, *It's time to go outside and shovel the driveway.* I'm thinking, *Remember to turn off the calf kidneys cooking on the stove.* I'm complimenting myself, *Yes, everything's handled. I can finish the steak and kidney pie when I come back inside.*

In this particular moment, I appreciate my unremarkable life and feel proud to hang onto these simple pleasures. Even going outside to shovel snow is a privilege.

I hold onto this thought as I head out the door. Suddenly, a shot of panic jolts my body like an icicle stabbing me in the back of the neck. Coming from nowhere, a question drills me with stunning brutality, *How can I live like this?* Under the ruthless scrutiny of this question, my life feels utterly useless. In a matter of seconds, any sense of assurance that I may have been feeling is obliterated and replaced with an overwhelming cold terror.

But despite this assault on my emotional equilibrium and

the automatic panic-response that follows, I detect a subtle difference this morning. The treachery of this unprovoked attack holds me hostage for a much shorter time. More importantly, I am able to fend off the sinister implications of the question, *How can I live like this?* that would otherwise contaminate every aspect of my life. Today, I am less desperate, more in control.

I begin wondering, *Does this slightly different reaction have anything to do with journalling? Is there something inherently powerful about writing from directly inside the experience, regardless of whether it's good, bad or ugly? Is there something inherently powerful about daring to talk about fears that riddle even the most innocent of pleasures? Does journalling help me withstand the process? Does each incident I encounter contribute to change over time, although the day-to-day pace is like that of snails, unbearably slow? Is this process similar to embroidering where each stitch, while appearing unimportant, contributes significantly to the finished whole?*

For months on end, I have wandered back and forth across the desert of a fabric landscape, a solitary nomad moving endlessly in the hope that there is value in what I do. In my embroidery and in my life, I recognize parallel processes. Neither is governed by reason and both require forbearance.

On the weekend, I began reading *Man's Search for Meaning* by Viktor Frankl and discovered that he would understand my own desperate drive for meaning. I take heart when he suggests that mental health is based on the tension between what *one is* and what one *is becoming*, between what *has been* achieved and *what remains* to be achieved. This echoes my own recent thoughts. With Frankl as a posthumous companion, I feel seen. Understood.

Suddenly, I'm protective of this new relationship and quick to silence that part of myself, which is outraged by my arrogance to speak of the two of us in the same breath. Me, from a place of relative affluence and certain safety, as opposed to Frankl who endured three horrendous years of imprisonment in Auschwitz. Shovelling snow today, I appreciate what it means to be working in the freezing cold. But unlike him, I am wearing fleece-lined boots and anticipating the pleasure of a hot cup of tea when I'm finished. I am unable to fathom being forced outside into sub-zero weather, barefoot and starving, to perform a meaningless task. Still, noting the places where his struggle and mine converge through distance and over time (if only ever so slightly), I feel grateful. Because of his story, my awareness becomes crystal-sharp.

My musings are interrupted by thoughts of the steak and kidney pie. I note how curious it is to see these domestic details lying so fearlessly close to the seemingly larger, life questions. Hot cereal on a cold morning, snow that needs shovelling, calf kidneys cooking on the stove, and existential angst. Strange bedfellows.

Body Work

In my dream I drive my car into a busy body shop that is also a barn. My car needs work. Inside, mechanics are covering cars with white paper to prepare them for resurfacing and painting. The men are sons of the tall woman who is in charge of the operation.

I ask her for a dozen free range eggs but when she brings them to me, I'm indignant. She's charging me $2.15 per dozen, which seems excessive. I wonder if I really need them. On the other hand, the work on my car will cost one thousand times more money than the eggs, which would provide excellent nutrition for my physical body.

After waiting some time, I ask one of the men where my car is and what's happening to it. He's surprised that I don't know that it's already in production and being repainted grey. I'm shocked and angry. No one has asked permission to do this. Besides, while I see that the existing paint job on my car (British Racing Green) is not perfect, it is still adequate. My car does not need body work. It needs a deep interior cleaning.

November 23, 1996 **Gibsons, British Columbia**

thwart \'thwȯrt *vb* to run counter to as to effectively oppose; to frustrate; to defeat the hopes or aspirations.

John calls this morning from Vancouver as I'm getting ready to leave for work at the project site. He's in a hurry—on his cell phone—on his way to talk to a group of women about his latest book. He also wants to tell me that he's reconnected with his former girlfriend, the woman he's lived with until a few months ago. He wants me to know where things stand between us so there won't be any expectations left hanging in the air. I appreciate his desire to set the record straight but his use of the word *reconnect* in this context feels coy to me, suggesting nothing short of an immaculate encounter. Suddenly I am furious.

Cut the crap, I want to say. *Why don't you just tell me directly, "We've decided to give it another try,"* instead of pussy-footing around?

It's OK, I want to say, *you can talk to me straight.* At the very least, I could take heart knowing that honest communication between men and women is possible. *I hate these damned games,* I want to say. But in the moment, hearing from him when I least expect, my response is devoid of feeling, my recovery delayed. I simply thank him for calling.

But when I get off the phone I find myself dealing with the tattered shreds of my own projections that are lying in a heap on the floor like tawdry Christmas tinsel. Functioning in the vacuum of my private fantasies, I have been creating an elaborate scenario of what I've called an adult Christmas: imagining myself on Christmas morning in bed with a lover, drinking champagne and eating smoked salmon on dark dense bread. But in the suddenly harsh light of my dashed desires, I find myself confronted with the unwelcomed knowledge of my single status. Back to square one again, man-wise, that is.

"How did that happen?" a voice asks. *"How did you get ahead of yourself with him already in your bed?"*

"Well," I retort defensively, *"there's no harm in imagining."*

"No, but how about a reality check first to see where he is in his life, to see what he really wants? I mean, did you take him into account, or was this mainly you, weaving a one-sided scenario? A kind of tunnel vision, with you zooming ahead with your own plans and projections?"

In a flash I'm presented with an answer to my question. My mind leaps to explain with a seasonal analogy and presents the image of a Christmas tree.

First, I see myselfbeholding the tree or as the analogy goes, the male object of my short-term intention, if not exactly long-term affection. Next, I begin decorating it, laying this bauble and that on the tree (or the man) without pausing to ask certain questions. *Is this how you'd like to see yourself decorated? Do my decorations match your vision of yourself?* Or on a final, more startling note, *Do you even want to be a tree?*

Already I'm sensing where a person could run amuck. Still, I comfort myself with the notion that this is precisely what men and women do when they meet each other. *"Isn't it?*

"Don't we all unconsciously decorate others with whatever qualities we wish to project onto them? Don't we all decorate them to match our ideal, until one day, when one or the other wakes up and says, "Hey, you've got it all wrong. This isn't me. This isn't how I want to be decorated. Besides, I'm not even an evergreen. I'm a much more fickle variety. I come and go as the seasons change."

But reflections aside, the status quo remains. I am still alone and despite the long drive to the site, by the time I set up my sales materials, my blood is still boiling. In my anger, I flash back to a recent incident that continues to infuriate me even as I'm sitting here in the sales office, writing in my journal. It unfolded like this.

Sarah and I were on our way to our choir practises, which are stacked, back-to-back, one hour after the other. Wedged between 3:30 when school's out and 5 o'clock when we have to be at practise, this is a quick turnaround time. As a treat for Sarah, I've agreed to take us to Wendy's for an early dinner. We've just put our trays down on the arborite table and seated ourselves on the hard disk-stools bolted to the floor when a woman whom I've met casually, whose daughter is about Sarah's age, comes up and asks, "Can we join you?"

"Sure," I say, "but we're only going to be here a few minutes."

A few minutes is all she needs. She takes my remark as an invitation to unload the emotional burden she's been carrying around for who knows how long, presuming, undoubtedly, because of our shared single status, that we must also share a similar jaundiced view of marriage and men. No doubt believing that she will find in me, if not sympathy, then at least empathy. Assuming that we are on the same sorry page, she seizes the moment and divests herself of tales about the injustices of being a single mom. As her litany unfolds, her energy increases exponentially. Her relief is palpable. Finally, she stops to catch her breath, leans towards me and asks, "Are you still on your own?"

My reaction is immediate: visceral and vile. My body tightens around a sudden surge of anger triggered by her question and the effort of stopping myself from lashing out at her. Instead of opening my mouth to say what's on my mind, I open my mouth to stuff in a sugar-coated doughnut hole, which I grab from the cardboard box in front of me.

Biting my tongue, I stop myself from spitting out the words, *Don't ever ask me if I'm 'on my own' again or this will be the last time I talk to you. Keep your poor-me story to yourself. And don't you ever refer to me again as a single mother of Gibsons—or SMOG as you cutely put it—or I'll rip your face off with my perfectly polished nails. And don't let the elegance fool you!*

Recalling this incident, I'm as furious as I was that day in the restaurant.

I hate everything, I mutter to myself. *Even this damned writing. Snivelling into my puny little book. Tell the truth. Say it!*

I want to be screwing my head off. Raking my red nails down your back—whoever you are—and holding you to my body until we're both worn and weeping. That's what I want.

In this moment of howling energy, I remember myself from years ago: a black feral cat, long legs and leather, claws and contained heat. The sharp edges of pain I'm feeling remind me that I'm still alive. My soul resonates with the wild beauty of the project site. I'm proud to be here alone with the rain smashing the windows, the waves hammering the shore, the ancient evergreens ratcheted by bitter winds. Proud to feel the return of my primal energies.

The elements, in their fierceness, mirror my own twisted rage-grief and at the same time, provide strangely sweet succour for my battered spirit.

I've blown the top off the container that has held my emotions like the canister of a bomb. I can finally breathe again. With the heat of suppressed feelings temporarily diffused, I'm suddenly curious about where this particular day falls within my now much-shortened monthly cycle. Not surprisingly, I discover that I'm smack in the middle of ovulation and the furious drive towards sexuality, release and regeneration.

I suspend my thoughts for a moment. *Here comes that fellow who owns the big condominum, walking towards the office. I wonder what he wants?*

December 11, 1996 **Gibsons, British Columbia**

tem•per **\'tem-pər** *vb* to bring to proper hardness and elasticity by successive heating and cooling; to make stronger and more resilent through struggle.

I open my eyes. The clock reads 5:52. *Am I awake, or is this just a blip before I fall back to sleep?* My mind sweeps over the inner landscape of my physical and emotional body for an update. Instant feedback: *No sign of a headache this morning. Refreshed.*

This is a huge relief. Immediately, I connect my sense of well-being to the gift of a solid night's sleep and a new magnetic pad for my bed that I recently broke down and purchased. Initially, I declined the saleswoman's offer to buy my own, hoping that the use of a courtesy pad for six weeks would be sufficient to restore my body to smooth sleeping order. But I was wrong.

The first night without the pad I was wracked with a familiar lurchy insomnia that had me waking, like a nursing mother, at roughly two-hour intervals: 2:10, 4:47. Within a week and desperate for sleep, I called the saleswoman and ordered one. "Just put it on my VISA," I told her. Once I had done the deed, despite the hefty price tag, I was well satisfied that I had bought myself the gift that keeps on giving.

Back to this morning, *stomach feels fine as well*, which is great news after a bout of diarrhea last week when I woke up suddenly in the middle of the night and realized that I was lying in a shitty mess. My revulsion in the moment was secondary only to my fear that I had ruined the borrowed mattress pad.

I revisit the nocturnal scene: see myself leaping out of bed, stripping off the bottom sheet to check whether I'd ruined the pad, washing myself off, and at the same time, fast-forwarding to an image of myself as an incontinent old woman. Impoverished, alone, and living the life of my worst fears in a basement suite. My only respite in endless days is watching the blur of feet hurry past my high basement windows and wondering, hope against hope, *Is someone coming to see me?*

I shudder at the thought, doubly disgusted, then pull myself back to the present. My mental meanderings and the ease at which I'm moving across a curious, early morning terrain, inform me, *Yes, I am awake.* With that information, I decide to get up and write in my journal.

6:15. The tea's made and steeping in the pot. I'm sitting at my dining room table, ready to write. Returning to my pencil and paper after a three-week absence is like returning to a lover. I allow myself to drop into a place of pleasure—deep, exquisite and quiet—and connect with an intrinsic sense that all is well. *This morning I am certain that somewhere in the subterranean regions of my being, there is movement; certain that something is happening. Glory be, the river flows!*

From what has been the barren vista of my existence, I detect the phantom shape of things to come, as yet only hinted at in the most ephemeral of terms but substantial enough for me to take note and count my blessings. My job at the sales office, for instance. I now recognize that it not only provides me with structure in a relatively unordered life, but it also gives me what Julia Cameron calls "a date with myself" every weekend.

Days on the project site keep me pleasantly occupied: reading and writing, interacting with prospective customers, and presenting the beautiful property. Without pushing the river (God knows I've tried), things appear to be emerging naturally from the chaos of unknowing. A bold trust replaces the cowering doubt and allows me to utter the words, *"Qué será, será... whatever will be, will be,"* without fearing that I will drop off the face of the earth. Gradually, I am beginning to sense that this journey is more an organic process of waiting for new growth to occur than it is a mechanical task of getting from *here* to *there.*

Reading-wise, I've been whetting my thirst for self-knowledge, enjoying a series of short-term, satisfying relationships with each author in the brief span of time that it takes to finish reading a book. Catering to inner and outer tastes, they range from commerce and career to soul and consciousness: *Boom, Bust & Echo: How to Profit from the Coming Demographic Shift; To Build the Life You Want: Create the Work You Love; Care of the Soul: A Guide for Cultivating Depth in Everyday Life* and *Dancing in the Flames: The Dark Goddess in the Transformation of Consciousness.* Each of these books has helped me reconsider my ideas about life and livelihood as I go about the task of rebooting myself personally and professionally.

The training I've recently completed to earn certification in teaching leadership skills has started me thinking about core competencies in the personal sense as well. I have been attempting to identify those activities that thrill me, that energize me, that take me into *kairos* time where nothing exists but the task at hand. I postulate: *If these are the things that I love, then these are the things that I must build my life around.* Passion, therefore (and not practicality), becomes the criteria for creating a life. *A life of soul.*

What am I passionate about? The question nails down my focus. First, I count creativity of any sort: writing and fibre arts, which allow me to explore my inner processes; decorating and refurbishing homes, turning neglected properties into valuable assets; teaching through a synthesis of ideas, pulling diverse threads of academic, spiritual and energetic traditions into lively unique models.

I am passionate about dreams and believe that each one is a gift to be cherished. I am also passionate about being a counsellor, which allows me to serve as a mirror to help my clients claim a fuller sense of self. I am passionate about the subtleties of the smallest unit of expression: the shades of distinction between one thread or another, one word or another. And I am wild about symbols, metaphors and meaning, a passion that is awakened suddenly when as a twelve-year-old girl in English class, I am introduced to the magical world of figurative language. Hearing about poetic devices for the first time, I recognized their potency immediately and fell instantly in love with the forms.

6:55. I have achieved something considerable. *By defining what I love, I have made what I love real.* Now that these ideas exist as words on paper, I can touch them as readily as I can grasp the polished marbles in a purple Crown Royal pouch. Like a colourful cat's eye or a cool steelie, these are prized possessions that I am willing to share, but unwilling to trade.

December 13, 1996 **Gibsons, British Columbia**

herald \ˈher-əld *vb* to announce, proclaim the approach of; to greet with enthusiasm, to publicize.

Like Demeter, the Greek goddess who wanders the earth desperately searching for her lost daughter, I have been wandering in the wilderness for years, mourning the loss of a younger self. When I finally begin to turn towards home, I am no longer the Athena woman whose vision is fixed on external affairs and outer appearances. My time in the wilderness has softened me. On good days, I am less concerned about the creeping signs of age—the telltale brown spots on my hands, the loosening skin tone on my inner thighs, or the beginning of a crepey neck—and am more interested in tending the fires of my inner life.

What holds my attention these days is a sense of quiet exhilaration: a feeling of expectancy that something momentous is being born. My work lies in the underground caverns of my being where I observe myself in the process of change. In the slowing down, the sloughing off of driving ambition, I gain pleasure in the moment, noticing and celebrating the tiny, day-to-day triumphs that announce my returning well-being. The familiar presence of anxiety reverberating throughout my body in continuous shock waves has all but disappeared. I feel more cohesive and increasingly able to enjoy delightful forays into fun and silliness. Music has returned to my life.

On a recent excursion into Vancouver I walk directly into the Magic Flute music store and inform the owner, "It's been years since I've bought any music and I need help. I think I'd like some piano music or maybe some cello." I accept his suggestion and soon find myself sitting at my own private music station, earphones on my head and indulging in a musical feast like a guest at a banquet. *Maybe I'll try a little of this. And now would you bring me a little of that?* This is nothing unusual for the man; he obliges happily.

I leave the store forty-five minutes later with a John Friesen piano and cello CD in my bag, feeling like a million dollars. I pause outside for a minute and wonder, *What should I do next?* My eyes light upon a window display of flannelette nightgowns and pyjamas in the lingerie store next door. I walk in, rifle quickly through the rack marked *Winters in Whistler* and select a bright red nightshirt that I can use for weekends away instead of bothering to pack a bulky robe. With the aplomb of a seasoned shopper, I lay down my VISA card, purchase the nightshirt without a second thought, and leave the store almost euphoric with my worldliness.

Suddenly, a sarcastic voice slices through my joy, "*Where have you been all this time that making two simple purchases should be such a big deal?*"

Alarm surges through my body but I withstand the sharp criticism and reply evenly, "*I've been in the land of the dead. But what's important is that I'm now alive!*"

Like the girl I saw in a recent dream who, although presumed dead, suddenly threw off the shroud she had been lying under for years. Once the bindings that had hobbled her feet were removed, she sat up, swung her legs off the marble mortuary slab, and rose. Frozen in time, which is only possible in dreams or cryogenics, she returned to life when the moment was right, lively and well like our goldfish who wait out the winter under a sheet of ice on the garden pond.

This morning I find pleasure in reflecting upon the steps I've taken to point myself in a new direction. I've been certified to teach a parenting program. I'm talking to a local television producer about an idea for a show called *Heart of the Matter* that would feature on-air counselling. I've finished my embroidery, which I've called *The First Night: Integration of the Masculine and Feminine*, and I'm talking to the local hospice society about developing a workshop using creativity as a response to grief. I've noticed, as well, in the course of these conversations, interesting energy developing between myself and one of the male directors.

Heeding the promptings of the Winter Gardener, I have been scattering seeds in all directions, alternating between times when I reach out to make contact with potential business clients, and periods of solitude when I read, write and reflect—allowing ideas to germinate in the stillness of my life—without the pressure I would normally impose upon myself to produce immediate results. Instead, I watch with curiosity, wondering, *Which idea will show itself as the first green shoot to push through the earth? Which idea will start strong, but fade quickly?*

The garden I now envision as my life is loosely-formed—growing and re-seeding itself, flourishing and dying off according to its natural rhythms—without meddling on my part, and *not* without weeds. A riot of colour, fragrance and variety: brown-eyed susans, purple flag irises, dark delphiniums, mauve and white heather, pink foxgloves, pale sweet peas, yellow, white and blood-red roses, scarlet clematis, pansies the colour and texture of queens' dresses, and lily-of-the-valley, delicate and white against the dark wet earth of spring.

"Why can't we have a pretty garden," Sarah complains one day, "and one without weeds?"

"Because," I reply, "I like my gardens wild."

Without conscious effort on my part, issues that have been incubating for months, maybe years, become suddenly clear. In a matter of an hour of clear-headed thinking, the shape of an intelligible picture emerges where once there were only random pieces. I see that this is the right time to sell a property that Joann and I own in Arizona. (When will the US/Canadian exchange rate be more favourable?) This is also the right time to turn the six hundred square feet of gaping space that Brian used as his office into something more useful—like an office for myself—instead of leaving it as a constant reminder of my loss like a missing front tooth. This is the right time for me, *Custodian of Family Effects*, to clear out the spa room, returning three decades' worth of personal and legal files to Brian and finally converting the room back into its original use.

Time to shed the misty veils of the Lady of Shallot and get a life. Time to leave the half empty house on the hill. Time to forget about tending the one-third acre property with its wild gardens and fruit-bearing trees, and time to scrap the tedium of sleeping alone in my king-sized bed.

It's time to buy a new bed. One that doesn't whisper of lovers long gone.

Decisions are wrought painlessly with the dispassion of a

flashing blade cutting away the old and making way for the new. Ideas collide and converge in blinding succession: old files, new furniture; future lovers and raging hormones.

But without a lover and feeling an animal-ache for sex, I take some satisfaction from knowing that I haven't wasted my energy entirely, but have harnessed it to make some important decisions.

Today I hail the return of a different sort of woman: a woman in one of her final moon cycles, still hungry for new life. A woman on the cusp of Sophia, the archetype of mature feminine wisdom, leaving behind the remnants of *what has been* and walking towards her power.

Tip of the Pain

In my dream I have been taken into an examination room for observation. There is no evidence of injury but I feel sharp pain below my right knee. When I bend down closely, I see the glint of a shard protruding through the skin, but those examining me neither see it nor believe me when I complain about the pain. Finally, a male doctor arrives and sees the shard immediately. Working quickly, he extracts a huge crystal from my knee.

Later I'm in a hospital bed and being observed once again. As before, I complain of discomfort and pain but no one believes me. Finally the doctor returns to the room, lifts up the sheet and makes a startling discovery. I am lying in hundreds of shards that have been expelled from my body. We are both astonished to see one particularly large shard lying along the right side of my body. Measuring about eighteen inches in length, it is jagged, heavy and shaped like a yoke. Like the other shards, this, too, has been buried in my body although I was unaware of its existence until now. The doctor treats me with respect and compassion. The discovery of these shards brings dignity to my suffering.

December 21, 1996 **Gibsons, British Columbia**

ex•press \ik-'spres *vb* to subject to pressure so as to force something out; to reveal; to put into words, to state directly.

I stand at the sliding glass door in my dining room. After four days the snow is still falling; the weather is the worst it's been in seventy-five years. Floppy flakes twist and turn, flying in a frenzied sideways motion. I look eastward towards the ocean below my home, waiting for the B.C. Ferries Queen of Surrey to come into view, to pull along the shoreline before turning abruptly and swinging out into Howe Sound. As if in a trance, I look upon this moving landscape, slowed down after a flurry of activity over the past two days getting Sarah ready to go away for her Christmas holiday. The rush is now over; Sarah is on the ferry with her dad and his new partner, Mary. I clutch my body in an instinctive gesture to comfort myself, wrapping one arm tightly around my torso and reaching with my other hand to touch my throat which is constricting and beginning to ache. Tears remain lodged somewhere in my body.

The scene bears similarities to another scene dating back two-and-a-half years: a gentle evening in June when Sarah and I watched the same ferry sweep her father, the man whom I had loved, away and out of sight towards Horseshoe

Bay and his recently-rented furnished suite on Denman Street in Vancouver. We explained to her that living in the city would be easier for him than spending so much time travelling back and forth between Vancouver and the Sunshine Coast.

That night she stood quietly at my side watching the ferry lights disappear, then slipped her small hand into mine and remarked, "It's almost as if Papa doesn't live here anymore," her comment finally articulating what Brian and I had been unable to say: that we were no longer living together.

From that time on, whenever he returned home, he slept in the downstairs bedroom. Our rooms, my upper and his lower, were connected by a heat vent through which Sarah would call down to him in the morning, "Wake up, Papa."

Today, I watch from behind the same wide expanse of window that invites me to peer through and imagine Brian, Mary and Sarah together, a small happy group leaving for the holidays. At the same time, I am aware that the window shuts me out. The glass is an impenetrable barrier; I can no longer reach those on the other side. I am spending Christmas at home while the three of them, now a family of a new configuration, are spending Christmas in Edmonton with Brian's family. With Brian and Mary undoubtedly occupying the same blue bedroom that he and I shared on previous years. With Brian and Mary undoubtedly sleeping in the same bed where, only last year, he slept alone while I slept in his brother's old bedroom in one of the soft single beds next to Sarah.

The occasion marked the last time that we were in Edmonton together as a family. We still had not told his parents that we were separated. Instead, we let our sleeping arrangements convey their own unhappy truth. Over the three days that we were there, the physical discomfort of a mushy mattress was preferable to the continuing pretence that things were fine between us. We had been living apart for a year-and-a-half, he with another woman. The dance of deception was wearing thin.

By the time we were ready to leave, Sarah wanted to stay a few extra days with her grandmother, which was fine with Brian and me. It did not change our plans. We intended to fly back to Vancouver together, pick up my car at the airport, and drop him off at his Denman apartment. After that I would catch the 7:30 ferry home. But events finally forced us to confront our personal situation directly.

Like tiny gashes cut into my memory, the details remain vivid as if etched in glass. We arrive at his apartment, already pressed for time. Trying to hurry, we open the trunk and separate luggage and gifts. Brian, rustling in various zippered pockets, looks for his house keys. He finds them and announces triumphantly, "Aha, I've got them!" In the meantime, I've locked myself out of my car which sits idling in the alley behind his apartment.

The moment I realize that I'm locked out, I realize that I'm locked out in a metaphorical sense as well. Locked out of my car, which I interpret from many dreams to be my ego vehicle or the means by which I am identified in the world, I am figuratively locked out of my marriage as well. My place is now usurped by another woman. As if to make sure that I understand the message in the starkest terms, the universe conspires to have Mary in the apartment when Brian brings me inside to phone for a tow truck to come and unlock my car.

Events occur in slow motion. Brian opens the door to his apartment. I step inside, smell soup cooking on the stove. Mary appears unexpectedly, like a Christmas elf. A surreal moment. We hesitate, two wary creatures. I move towards her, opening my arms and reaching out to embrace her. *Her body is entirely different than mine.*

A strange thought surfaces, *What are they like in bed?* Brian watches immutably from the kitchen, next to the pot of soup.

Somehow the three of us, individually and collectively, manage to gather together sufficient wits to remain hospitable in each others' presence for another ten minutes. Mary asks "Would you like some soup?" I balance a bowl on my knees while Brian, looking glazed, manages only the occasional barely-audible comment. At last, I'm about to be delivered from this unnatural situation.

The intercom sounds, announcing the arrival of the truck driver. Brian buzzes him in. He appears at the door, asks to see my membership card, and leaves to work on my car. This is my signal. I stand up to go, make my way towards the door, walk down the hall and out past the EXIT sign to my red car, which is now unlocked and ready for me.

I open the car door and step inside. Settle myself in the seat. Snap on my seat belt. Roll up the driver's window, snug and tight. The vehicle, now sealed, becomes a safety container for my tightly-held feelings.

A distant thought registers, *I've had enough. I can't think anymore. Get me out of here.*

I shift the car into reverse and pull out of the driveway. At the same time, I pull a blanket of detachment over myself that I will use to comfort me for the better part of a year—until the muffled sounds of my pain pierce through the protective covering.

By last summer, I realized that the only way I could deal with my mounting feelings of terror, loss and dread, was to confront them directly.

I return to the present, December 1996. Standing at the same window and looking out towards the ocean, I am forced to admit once again that I am no longer impervious to my pain.

December 26, 1996 **Gibsons, British Columbia**

ex•pand \ik-'spand *vb* to describe fully or in detail; to throw off reserve; to open out; to swell, dilate.

Today is Boxing Day, five days after my tremendous let-down when Sarah left for Edmonton. It is also the day after a surprising turn of events. From my seat on the sofa, I watch the light change to a soft grey of late afternoon. Objects lose their sharpness of line and colour, take on a less specific form. The mood becomes reflective; it invites me to pause and savour. I scan the details of the past day and a half as if they are captured in my mind's eye on slow-speed film.

I remember the champagne that I opened last night and jump up to pour myself what's left from the bottle (not more than half a glass, but still fizzy and delicious), then return to the living room and settle down happily to review the recent events. With an imaginary flick of a finger, I can push whatever button I choose. Pause, Stop, Fast Forward, Rewind. I mentally press Rewind and wait for the film footage to return to the beginning, to yesterday and Christmas morning. I press Play.

Awakening without the jarring sound of the alarm, I immediately feel the luxury of the day. After a long soak in the tub, I light candles of various size, shape and fragrance throughout the house, intentionally leaving the lights off. The rooms take on a shimmery magical quality. I sit with Nala nestled on my lap and make long-distance calls while I admire my twinkling tree—twinkling because earlier this week I inadvertently bought a string of lights with a twinkle chip when I thought I was buying a plain clear set like my others. Still, the effect is delightful.

Next, I change my bedding, stripping off my everyday sheets and duvet cover and replacing them with the beautiful bedding I found ten years ago at an antique furniture sale, in the bottom drawer of a chest. Knowing that I had found a treasure, I purchased the whole set immediately: the sheet, the hand-cut embroidered duvet cover and pillow cases. Since then, this set has been reserved for special occasions: birthdays, anniversaries, Valentine's Day, Christmas.

I lift the cotton bedding from the closet and run my hands thoughtfully over the crisp fabric. As an embroiderer, I can appreciate the time, as well as the intense discipline and love, required to complete this work. Unmistakably bed linens created for a wedding night, a cupid stands in a floral setting, holding up a banner which trumpets wishes for the intended couple, *Amore.*

Yet when I discovered this antique bedding, the white fabric was still full of sizing, suggesting that it was never used. As I slip my down quilt into the duvet cover and shake it vigorously to fluff it out, I find myself wondering, *What unforseen events, decades ago, robbed the bride and her groom of the promise of their wedding night?* The mystery and the beauty of the handmade items heightens my pleasure as I create a sensuous bedroom which I may, or may not, share with a lover.

By 3:00 in the afternoon, I'm dressed and ready to leave for Davis Bay, a small community about fifteen miles up the coast from my home. I'm having dinner with friends from Calgary. Before going to their house, however, I'm picking up Garth, the man from the hospice society, whom I've invited to join us for Christmas dinner. Conveniently, he lives only two blocks from our destination. *Old friends, new friends and a white Christmas!*

I pull into Garth's driveway, climb out of the car, knock on his door, and wait for him to open it. Seeing him, I blurt out nervously, "My God, I'm feeling awkward."

Over the course of the evening, I'm acutely aware of his presence. My nervousness has dissipated. Instead I am feeling a strong sexual attraction towards him. He, on the other hand, shows no particular interest in me. Feeling frustrated, I drive him back to his house after dinner.

Parked in the driveway, I recognize *a now or never* moment. Suddenly, I'm less concerned about maintaining social niceties—we've had those all evening—than I am in speaking the truth. I remind myself to allow him a gracious way out yet at the same time, I want to be perfectly clear. I turn to him, plunge in directly and say, "I'd like to make love with you."

"You would?" he says, fumbling for a moment before recovering and catching the pass. "Well, then, drive me home with you. I'll find my way back here tomorrow."

Now it's my turn to fumble. Even though it was I who threw the pass, his response feels sudden, unexpected. With a pronounced sigh of relief, I feel the tension slide off my body. I slump momentarily against the car door, using the unyielding metal frame to support my resolve. The long drive home is a godsend. Like exquisite foreplay, it allows time to heighten my excitement and help me process these events.

When we arrive home, I turn to him in the car and say, “Let me go in first. I need five minutes, then you can come in.”

As I stand at my red front door, a Christmas wreath made from our own grapevines welcomes me. Plaid ribbons, fresh sprigs of holly and red feather birds add a festive flavour to the seasonal greeting. I unlock the front door and step into the foyer. I pull out a box of wooden matches from the hutch drawer and begin lighting a succession of candles. I start with red oversized pillars standing in wrought iron pedestal holders, then dash upstairs to light a long row of green candles flanking the mantle.

Finally, I move down the hallway and into my bedroom where I light a pair of stout gold beeswax candles sitting in ornate holders on either side of a large mirror, finishing with the small votive candles on my bedside tables.

The bedroom is a pool of light and reflection. I glance at my bed, my eyes resting briefly on the wide expanse of fresh white linen, the pile of pillows stacked on the bed, and the small embroidered figure enjoining us playfully to *love*. My home is ready. I return downstairs, wave to Garth from the front door and call out, “OK, you can come in now!” I usher him into the foyer; the home envelops us in sensory pleasure.

In my mind’s review I slow down the film to recapture each successive frame more fully, knowing that this occasion marks an important milestone.

Once we’re upstairs, I leave Garth to light a fire in the living room while I pop open the bottle of champagne that I’ve left chilling in the fridge. We sit on the sofa drinking champagne and listening to Placido Domingo and the Vienna Choir Boys sing their favourite Christmas carols. Finally, I announce, "I'm exhausted."

"Well, then, let's go to bed," he says, standing up and starting to move towards the bedroom. I retrace my steps, blowing out the same candles that I lit an hour earlier, until the only remaining light is from the fire in the grate, which will burn itself out during the night. The house is silent and dark except for my bedroom, which is a warm oasis beckoning two weary travellers.

Making love with this man, I encounter an essential part of myself that has been buried under heavy wraps for too long. My days without lovemaking have heightened my awe for the pleasure I'm feeling. I am an innocent and a woman who has been here before. I open myself to this man in my arms, in my bed, in my home. I open myself to the beauty of this moment: the taste, the touch, the smells. *This is where I want to be.*

A candle burns low, flickers, gasps and dies. The thick gold candles drip heavy clots of wax onto my mother's old lace runner. I blow them out.

This morning, the morning after, I awaken ahead of him. I slip quietly out of bed, prepare fresh fruit, put on a pot of coffee and wait for him to get up. At the same time, I quietly relish the pleasure that I've experienced over the past few hours, recalling certain words, gestures, sounds.

Later as we sit over breakfast and just before he leaves, I say, "I want to show you something." I go over to where I've left my recently-finished embroidery, pick it up and pass it to him.

He bends over and studies it closely, then remarks, "This is really beautiful."

Content to simply show him my work, I do not try to explain the deeply personal meaning of *The First Night: Integration of the Masculine and Feminine*. I do not explain that the work, completed in the darkness of late fall, articulates a profound passage in my inner journey. Or that it held the power to compel me forward when I might otherwise have ceased my *winter gardening*. Nor do I explain that it marks the first night in over ten years that I've slept with a man other than Brian.

Instead, I keep my reasons for celebration to myself, knowing that after hundreds of hours, hundreds of stitches, and hundreds of nights alone, I have created *the first night*.

I come to the end of my review; press the imaginary Stop button. The film's in the can!

January 21, 1997 **Gibsons, British Columbia**

shrink \'shrink *vb* to grow smaller; to contract or curl up the body; to recoil instinctively; to lessen in value.

Almost a month after Christmas, I finally return to my writing and begin to sort out the shambles I've been dealing with since Garth left Boxing Day morning saying, "I'll call you in a day or so. Right now I want to spend some time with my sons."

Lulled into a false sense of security because he's spent Christmas with me, and imagining that we had started a relationship, I am assured by his parting remark. I fully expect to hear from him again, but I don't. As I wait for a call, tension begins to insinuate itself in my body. Nights bring only patchy sleep, intermittent one and two-hour shots of relief. My distress increases with each successive day he doesn't call. One sleepless night builds upon another.

An earthquake has flattened the tenuous ground around me. I survey the ruins asking myself, *What the hell happened?* The shame of being left high and dry mixes insidiously with painful memories. I recall the pain of an incident eleven years ago before I was married. Brian was out with another woman; I was trying to retain my sanity—wandering around a dimly-lit parking lot looking for his car, planning to throw rocks through the windows. The two occasions are separated by years but similar in the way I try to rein in the fierce feelings assaulting my body and not being particularly successful.

My thoughts return to New Year's Eve, which mocks me with its promise of new beginnings. I avoid it entirely, cowering under the bed covers and thrashing about in the minutes leading up to, and over, the midnight hour.

The following morning is New Year's Day. Before leaving for a psychotherapy training on Vancouver Island and in a burst of uncontrolled emotion like a woman at the wailing wall, I sweep through the house and ravage it of any vestige of Christmas. I tear down candles, wreaths, decorations and the tree that I've promised Sarah I won't take down until she returns from Edmonton. Through it all, I am fully aware that I will have to contend with her inevitable anger sooner or later. Yet this is something I need to do. Paring the Christmas clutter from my house creates a semblance of order. To mitigate the damage I'm wreaking in terms of her trust of me, I leave the tree standing upright in its metal base and banish it to the outside deck.

But once the decorations are down, I start to wrestle with my resistance to leaving for the training. I notice my fears surfacing and recognize that I'm trying to negotiate my way out of this commitment. *Why does it have to be so far from home? For so long? And it's always so damned intense. Maybe I can opt out of this one.* I want nothing more than to cling to the comfort of my own four walls and close out the world-at-large.

But time marches on; the ferry demands that I adhere to its rigid schedule. Finally, I pack a bag, grab a handful of books, grab my purse and coat and lock the door behind me, virtually prying myself out of the house.

Throughout the week I hunker down, trying to keep my emotions at bay and concentrate on the challenging material. I'm intent on applying what I'm learning in this couples' therapy workshop to my own situation. At the very least, I might gain some perspective on why I've been attracted to Garth.

In terms of energy and character style, he's very similar to my father. Both share a fierce sense of duty, a black and white outlook on life, as well as a cool rational way of dealing with matters. Even the body—tall, slim and well-toned—is familiar. Of course I would gravitate to him. I recognize him in my bones. But in terms of creating a relationship with him, I now see the folly of my thinking. Ironically, I got precisely what I wanted: a man with whom to share a sexy Christmas.

Reconnecting with Sarah after the training is the only bright spot in a painful stretch of time, although I still have to face her anger for breaking my promise. As it happens, she accosts me one morning while she's in her bathroom brushing her teeth and while I'm standing behind her, looking into the mirror and drying my hair. "You said you wouldn't take down the tree or decorations until I got home and I'm very mad at you." Her eyes force me to look directly at her in the large mirror.

"You have a right to be angry with me," I reply, "I gave you my word and then I did it anyway." I pause for a moment, then continue, "I'm very sorry. I know how broken promises feel."

I'm anxious to mend this breach of trust and stay home with her but I'm scheduled to be away again soon, this time for a course that will certify me to present parenting programs as an independent facilitator in my community.

The course material turns out to be excellent and I am optimistic that it will become a solid piece of work upon which I can stand professionally. *Perhaps it will open a path through the career maze I find myself in.* Like fresh-laid sod cutting through the thick brambles in front of me, the possibilities for this work appear lush and welcoming.

On the other hand, once the course is over, I can't wait to check out of the Stay and Save Motor Inn, climb into my car, and drive back to my home on the Sunshine Coast.

I am stuck in the doldrums and this is *winter gardening* at its worst.

Delayed Flight

In my dream I am waiting at home for a flight that has been delayed for more than a day. After the delay, I am checking in again at the airport. I have my ticket and the plane will take off shortly. The flight attendant, whose surname is Newman, is also a counsellor and a teacher. Seeing someone I recognize assisting on this flight, I feel calm and confident. I know that I will find emotional support.

February 8, 1997 **Vancouver, British Columbia**

lean \ˈ**lēn**\ *vb* to incline in opinion, taste, or desire; rely on for support or inspiration.

The past three days I've been at the Vancouver Boat Show, representing the condominium project where I work. Between 10:00 in the morning and 10:00 in the evening I staff the booth that is housed in a massive concrete trade centre handing out sales brochures, Chamber of Commerce information on the Sunshine Coast, and trying to stay warm while talking to prospective customers.

"Where *is* this place?" they ask, despite the fact they're often looking directly at a large laminated map with a red arrow indicating THE SITE. Like the map itself, most of these exchanges are cardboard conversations between strangers following a predictable series of questions and answers. Still, the long weekend is not without its triumphs. The satisfactions, however, have less to do with boats than with beauty.

During the show I'm staying with my aunt in North Vancouver. Denise, a friend from Calgary, is also staying with us. At the end of each day, I close up the booth and drive across the Lions Gate Bridge to the north shore. After my aunt goes to bed, Denise and I pick up the threads of conversations from previous nights, often gravitating to the topic of struggling to find our niche at this time in our lives.

"How can two women, apparently bright, well-educated and energetic be so lost?" Denise muses aloud, standing in the small kitchen and passing me a glass of chilled chardonnay before pouring one for herself.

Picking up her drift, I continue, "And how can two women who have experienced success in most things we've touched, find ourselves—like you at forty-four and me at forty-nine—uncertain and shakey, without a clue as to what we're doing?"

"When I think about how confident I used to be ...," her voice trails off wistfully.

"Can you believe it," I offer, swinging emphatically into my own example, "I used to be the golden souffle. And now it's a struggle to even look at myself in a store mirror."

We exchange knowing looks.

"Well," I continue somewhat forcefully, "I want to tell you, my conversations with you are food for my soul. You have no idea what a relief it is to admit these things. To laugh and cry with someone."

Each of us takes a sip of wine, reflecting quietly on this recent round of disclosures.

"Hey, I've got an idea," she suggests brightly. "Why don't we get our make-up done? Buy some new cosmetics? We could go on your way to the boat show tomorrow."

After a brief discussion, we conclude that London Drugs is where we will have the greatest chance of seeing our task through to completion, our reasoning being that the women in the cosmetic departments of either Holt Renfrew or The Bay are too young, too beautiful, too perfect.

"I'd feel like slapping their flawless faces," I remark as I imagine the prospect of finding myself in that situation.

Friends with a common goal, the following morning we embark on this next piece of personal work, bolstering each other's confidence as we approach the counter. Hesitating for a moment, we huddle together, speaking in hushed conspiratorial tones, considering who we want to talk to. Will it be Colleen, who looks roughly our age but it's hard to tell with the skillful application of make-up, or will it be Wendy, slightly pudgy and clearly younger? We settle on Colleen. We approach her together. Denise takes the aesthetic initiative by the horn and announces, "We need your help."

"You don't look like you need help," is Colleen's quick comeback.

Good start. We've established a mutual respect; now we can get to work. In no time, we've tossed our outdated products—foundation, eye shadow, liners and lipstick—into the garbage can on the basis that the tones are too harsh. By this time, we've removed whatever make-up we applied this morning with Colleen's creamy cleanser and stand figuratively naked, taking turns considering ourselves in the fluorescent mirror.

Seeing myself in this stark light of reality, I groan inwardly, *Do I continue this, or do I slide out, right here and now?* Colleen has slipped in close beside me and is scrutinizing my magnified face. Silently we take stock: enlarged pores, age marks, blotches, yellowish skin with red overtones.

"Those tiny veins are broken capillaries," she comments helpfully. "We can find a nice foundation to cover them. Also, you can use a mild exfoliant once a week to slough off the dead skin."

Colleen is now in full stride. Denise and I watch with

admiration as she applies dabs of liquid foundation along our jaw lines; flicks on blusher with an 'up and outwards towards the eye' motion; peels off and sticks onto the back of her hand, strips of clear scotch tape and then applies colour after colour of lipstick shades. We catch her momentum; we are emboldened, responding to each successive product with comments such as, "There's too much blue in it. Too much red, get rid of it!"

Our speech, spiked with old-man words like *ruddy, sturdy, portly,* gives voice to our barely-concealed dismay that a woman should be expected to remain beautiful forever. We rely upon our laughter like a crutch to keep us from falling into our shame and limping away from the whole ugly matter. Armed with humour, we beat back the spectre of becoming old and invisible from this moment forward.

Our venture takes on epic proportions. We stand together, two quixotic female figures, bemused and somewhat sad. Our former Athena selves are no longer resplendent in golden armour; our clothes, as metaphors, need reshaping and refashioning. The figurative shields we once carried to render us emotionally invulnerable have disappeared. The spotlights under which we thrived have softened. Our sense of self is likewise diffused. Through it all, insecurities surrounding body and being are laid bare.

I leave the store feeling almost giddy with my bag of cosmetics, knowing that I've had a breakthrough of sorts. By throwing out my old make-up and choosing more suitable products, I've also thrown out some beliefs about myself. A voice admonishes me gently, "*You don't owe it to anyone to be beautiful.*"

As I unlock my car door, I ask myself, *Do I give a damn about any of this?* The answer is simultaneously *yes* and *no.*

No, if it means buying into someone else's notion of what I should be, whether it is a notion of beauty or of anything else. *Yes*, if it's an authentic expression of the woman I'm becoming.

March 7, 1997 **Gibsons, British Columbia**

thrust \ **'thrəst** \ *vb* to push or drive with force; to make one's way; to extend, spread, press onward.

Leaving behind the rain-drenched days of January and February, I take heart this morning, noticing the first signs of spring. The sound of swallows under my eaves, reminding me that I wasn't fast enough to stop them from returning and assuming proprietary rights in my home. The sight of crocuses and primroses dotting the dark earth in my garden with hopeful splashes of yellow, purple and mauve. The sight of green waxy tulips pushing through the soil, broadcasting their perennial exuberance for life.

In similar fashion, I break into new turf myself as I start to advertise and promote my first parenting course, which I've scheduled to begin in early April. Drawing upon my door-knocking and cold-calling skills from my commercial real estate days, I step out again. I talk to anyone who will talk to me: moms, dads, coaches, grandparents and ministers alike. I visit government agencies and hand out my flyers to social workers, mental health professionals, law enforcement officers, teachers, principals and school counsellors.

I cut a wide swath through the community as I work to generate excitement and enrollments for the course, trusting that my efforts will ultimately bear fruit and create income. Except for the meagre amount that I've earned from a sparse crop of clients, I have yet to make any real money since finishing my degree last July.

A new file, Business Development, sits on my desk and attests to my growing sense of assurance that things *will* start happening, *must* start happening, yet I still struggle with unexpected bouts of panic and self-doubt. I second-guess myself, *Am I spreading myself in too many directions?* or I worry, *Am I missing opportunities?* Like the other night, for instance.

As I stand in a movie line-up, a woman who is employed by the Ministry of Health & Welfare, turns to me and asks, "Are you going to the Narrative Therapy Conference?"

The question is harmless but the impact is huge. My stomach sinks; my head spins. I manage to mumble, "No, I'm not," hiding the fact that I didn't even remember the conference, although narrative is my preferred model of counselling. And despite the fact that it was I who initially brought narrative therapy workshops to the coast as a counselling intern.

Unravelling the meaning of this incident after I return home, I trace it to feelings of shame about not measuring up to some arbitrary level of professional performance. I suspect that the source of my trouble is Athena who raises hell with her impossible standards. Watching me take each tiny step towards building a new identity, she laughs contemptuously. Her scorn tempts me to apologize for failing to meet my own and others' imagined expectations. For being, as yet, unformed and incomplete: an amorphous shape, barely articulated.

Like the emperor awaiting new clothes, I stand naked.

And like his tailor, I continue to pull threads into existence as I design for myself a splendid new set of garments. Yet, until such time that these threads take on colour and substance, I stand too exposed to present myself with well-established professionals. It is no small wonder that I rejected the idea of attending this conference (if only unconsciously) the very moment I heard of it.

"No," I should have said in response to the woman's question, "I'm not ready to undergo your scrutiny to determine whether I meet your standards. I may never be, in fact."

In moments like these, I become aware of the tremendous energy required to propel a human being into orbit on an uncharted life course. The lift-off is no less challenging or uncertain than the lift-off of a rocketship. Both require the same enormous preparation, the same engineering of a vision into form with metal, nuts and bolts; with words, symbols and dreams. Drawing upon tons of reserve fuel, the craft (human or otherwise) is shot from the comfort of familiar terrain out beyond the earth's gravity to set itself free in the blue-sky territory of unlimited possibility. Compelled to undertake a mission of staggering proportions by nothing more than an urge—part intuition, part blind faith, part insanity.

March 22, 1997 **Gibsons, British Columbia**

stun \\'stən\\ *vb* to overcome with astonishment or disbelief; to make senseless, groggy or dizzy as of by a blow; to shock.

Where is my sister when I need her? In Mexico, probably in her roof garden. This morning I feel not only exhausted but also disoriented. Last night Cecelia called from Calgary to tell me the news that Claire, our friend and fellow teacher from St. Michael's Junior High where we taught school together twenty-five years ago, had just died. She had breast cancer a few years ago and thought she had beaten it. Ultimately, it reappeared in her spinal column.

Then in the middle of the night, at 4:05 to be precise, the phone rings. It's the purchaser for our Arizona property, calling to confirm the sale and tell me that he's wired the deposit funds.

"Do you know what time it is?" I ask, struggling to be coherent.

"Oh," he replies, nonplussed, "here in Minnesota, it's seven in the morning."

I climb out of bed at 6:30, feeling like I'm on planet Pluto. The news of Claire's death still vivid in my mind, I place a call to the Polley family in Ottawa to check on Mary Ellen, another friend who has been struggling with cancer. A brain tumour. Suddenly I'm alarmed. *Why didn't I hear from her this Christmas?*

Her husband answers the phone. Sparing me the details, he cuts to the bone, "Mary Ellen died in November."

I can barely breathe. The news, like bodies stacked one on top of another, haunts me, triggers thoughts of the dead girl in my dream who threw off her shrouds, rose up and walked. A chilling thought registers like a voice from beyond the grave. It reminds me, *They're not the only ones who have been dead.*

Huge pieces are missing from a puzzle that was once intact. I'm looking for the piece of the party scene—three of us, Claire, Mary Ellen and I stand with our arms draped around each other, grinning and laughing. I recall that I was leaving for a sailing trip to the Gulf Islands the next morning. A second piece is also missing—the two of us, Mary Ellen and I, celebrating her upcoming wedding the night before I left for a trip to Mazatlan. We drank too much wine. Still dizzy in the morning, I groped my way out of bed and into the shower. Running out the door, I grabbed a handful of parsley from the fridge, hoping that it would sweeten my boozy breath like I had once been told it would. All of us, irrepressible young women. A song from this same era filters into my mind, *"Where have all the flowers gone, long time passing? Where have all the flowers gone, long time ago?"*

Suddenly, I look at the time. I need to get moving if I don't want to be late for work.

I drive through the gates of the project and pull up in front of the sales office. My eyes travel towards the big condominium and notice a white 4 X 4 parked outside. It belongs to Colin, a bachelor in his late 40's who lives here part-time when he's not at his other home in Lions Bay, the same man who's been inviting me to go skiing. Finally, I decide to accept his invitation to Whistler, closing the gap on the five years that have lapsed since I skied. We make a date for the following weekend.

After the first few runs in the morning with Colin, I'm firmly planted back on my skis and pleasantly surprised to find that I've regained most of my balance, if not all of my confidence. Checking the time, we go into the lodge just after noon, as pre-arranged, to meet Brian and Sarah who are skiing this weekend with Brian's sister, Susan. *Colin might as well meet the whole family at once,* I think to myself as I introduce them.

Sarah's eyes open wide when she sees me with another man. This is a first for her. For all of us. We keep our time together intentionally brief. Finishing lunch, the five of us leave the lodge. Before heading off down the hill, we stop for a moment to discuss which run we'll take.

For a split second, my mind jams. The gears in my brain try to separate the conflicting messages. My body reacts with the conditioned response of a Pavlovian dog. It wants to follow Brian down the hill. *This is where I feel safe,* it protests. *This is the man I followed down the "steep and deep" runs of helicopter skiing.*

You can't do that, hisses my mind, *it's just not right.*

I can't disagree with its logic.

Colin starts down the run and I follow closely behind, matching his turns. Like tracks carved in fresh snow, the meaning of my choice is clear to all of us, including Sarah, who has fallen in line naturally behind Brian and Susan. After this single symbolic run, Colin and I ski off in another direction, leaving them with goodbyes and a wave.

My thoughts return to the dead girl in my dream. If I'm to make any meaning whatsoever of the death of my two friends, it's to recognize instinctively that it's time for me to come back to life.

April 12, 1997 **Gibsons, British Columbia**

launch **ˈlȯnch**\\ *vb* to spring forward; to get off to a good start; to hurl, discharge, release.

Like the birds who are still busy under my eaves, I've been cleaning my house these past few days, inside and out. I start by washing windows in the morning, catching the sun while it's still low enough in the sky to see the fine film of winter grime and yet warm enough to dry my Windex windows quickly. I finish much later in the day, working in my west-facing back yard. Often it's the fast-encroaching darkness that pushes me back into the house rather than a less urgent need like hunger. The lengthening days translate into more working hours and by the end of the day, the dirtier and more exhausted I feel, the happier I am. My spring cleaning rites are a purification of sorts, in preparation for Easter. As I prune and polish, heave and haul, mow and move, I marvel that the impasse of winter and the plodding despair is now behind me.

When I stop to consider what I've accomplished recently, I realize that it has *not* been a fallow time after all, despite what Athena might say. Keeping her at bay and looking at the long list I compile, I see evidence of solid results. As my garden takes on colour, so does my life. Within the joy from my labours is the promise of resurrection.

I count my accomplishments.

1) We've firmed up the sale of our Arizona property and will have the balance of our money by the first of July (not a day too soon).

2) I've had the roof replaced on Joann's house as a welcome home surprise for her. She can admire it when she's swimming in the ocean.

3) I've also refinanced the property to take advantage of falling interest rates and saved us $400 per month in the process!

4) I've been writing stories and reading them to my parenting class. The participants seem to love them. The personal anecdotes add colour to the material that we are studying and the course comes alive. Many of the stories add an element of hilarity: *All About Nits, Cultivating Gardens & Healthy Children, The Real Stuff, When The Cat's Away,* and *Three Limp Balloons.* The stories allow me to share my creativity and connect in more personal way.

5) A proposal to teach this same course has been accepted by a community college as part of its Fall '97 calendar. For me, this means a big boost to my credibility as well as professional affiliation.

6) I've been hired by the high school where I completed my counselling internship to design and deliver a workshop called *An Entrepreneurial Attitude Towards Life* for the Career and Personal Planning Program. This is a chance to earn some income and reconnect with many of the people I met during my three months at the school.

7) I've cleaned out closets and sent a huge pile of clothes and bedding (including sheets from Brian's and my bed) to an orphanage in Baja, California, supporting a team of local parishioners who are going there as volunteer workers.

8) I've had my hair cut short which makes me feel more visible.

9) I've bought two beautiful new outfits, one from my sister's store and the other, a silk knit Ralph Lauren skirt and linen jacket, reminiscent of the movie, *Out of Africa*. And after much deliberation (and matching the mood of my new outfits), I've also bought myself a new perfume called Safari.

10) I've made my singing debut—performing with my choir at the annual music festival. *This is stepping out* in yet another way.

The only discordant note on my list of satisfactions is tomorrow's upcoming meeting with Brian to hash over the financial terms of our separation agreement. I'm determined to untangle myself from an agreement I made with him several months ago. We had decided to establish a trust for Sarah, which would be managed jointly between Brian and me. The full realization of what I've agreed to do eludes me until one day when I am walking alone on the beach.

A voice challenges me, *"Needing your soon-to-be-ex-husband's permission before you can deal with your own asset? Your ex-husband scrutinizing your affairs, with the ability to stymie any decision, for whatever reason he might have? You need your head examined!"*

Dawning slowly and building quickly, my repugnance to the idea becomes full-blown alarm. Pressure in my chest; constriction in my breathing.

I need breathing space! My body recoils in anticipation of contending with this suffocating arrangement. The voice continues, *"No longer married, but encumbered by the conditions of a trust? Still joined at the hip, while receiving none of the benefits of marriage, nor any of the freedoms of divorce?"*

The whole scenario is as disgusting as a recent dream when I struggle to dislodge a thick clot of phlegm that is stuck in my throat. When it becomes obvious that my efforts to spit it out are futile, I resort to a pair of pliers and yank it out brutally. Clearly, I have things to discuss with Brian.

On a happier note however, I've spent some very pleasant time with Colin recently, skiing again and going into Vancouver for dinner. He's generous and attentive, easy to be with. And I'm not oblivious to the sexual energy I felt when I was in his new condominium last weekend, helping him hang pictures. Finding the perfect place for a pair of Picasso prints in the luxurious master bathroom, I didn't need a sketch to tell me I was awake, aroused and alive.

Let Us!

In my dream I'm in a large state-of-the-art kitchen with a lover who is happily chopping up several heads of romaine lettuce into cross-wise strips which resemble the size, shape and colour of dollar bills. I'm surprised; this is not how I would cut up the leaves. Soon there is a huge pile of lettuce money.

On a sudden impulse, I pick up the pile, toss it onto the floor, jump into the pile and roll in it, sharing a naturally erotic moment with my companion. Our connection is playful and sexy.

May 3, 1997 **Gibsons, British Columbia**

smoul•der \'smol•dər *vb* to burn inwardly or in a suppressed way without flame; to be consumed by anger, hate or jealousy.

Spring, the sensuous season, is upon us. I need to be outside this morning. Despite evidence that it rained last night, I plant myself down on the wet webbing of the deck lounge, happily indifferent to the clamminess I feel seeping through my clothing. Instead, I savour the luxury of the sixty-something degree morning. I inhale the scent of fruit blossoms; marvel at the sky, a tufted quilt of grey and blue patches; note the temperature of the air, warm with the slightest cool undertone. Nala sits in my lap and plies me with her coy feline charms, insisting that I admire and stroke her. Her thick golden coat is warm from the sun.

The May Sarton in me is torn between writing and gardening, between the desire to be still and the need to be physical. To dig, dance, move, make love, sing. Canada Geese honk overhead on their homeward flight. Like the geese, I'm restless to return to the ocean. *"I must go down to the sea again, to the lonely sea and the sky,"* if only to drag the old electric lawnmower down the steep wooden steps at Joann's home and mow the lawn before she returns from Mexico.

Her garden literally burst into life three weeks ago, transformed into a delightful show of exotic hues. The tulips I planted in January are still beautiful, although past their prime. Taller and more stately than most, their tones and textures are those of chocolate wax or clothes in a costume trunk, rich and satiny. Still others, parrot tulips, dress themselves in soft fuschia tones, their shaggy edges and veins outlined in gay chartreuse.

Veins. The blood in my veins is heating up. I long to strip naked and tan my entire body, which I will do next spring when Sarah and I travel to Mexico with Joann. There, in her roof-top garden, I'll welcome the sensory pleasures surrounding me: orange and red bougainvillaea climbing wildly along the garden wall, opulent roses in sturdy, hand-painted Mexican pots, blue jacaranda blossoms, the scent of white jasmine. The beauty intoxicating me; the sun healing me—body, mind and spirit.

Body. Body heat like I witnessed yesterday when I was back at the high school to deliver my workshops. The three morning sessions moved along uneventfully; the afternoon, however, was a different matter.

The bell rings to announce the beginning of the class and a pack of grade eleven students tumbles in, led by a fellow (recently released from juvenile detention) named Buzz.

Buzz stakes claim to a seat on the saggy floral sofa at the back of the room *(Since when have there been sofas in classrooms?),* accompanied by his very pretty girlfriend. He drapes his long arm over her bare thigh, his hand beginning to move in a lazy motion up and down her leg. The bold demonstration of their easy sexuality staggers me. I struggle to introduce my topic, asking the students self-reflective questions such as, "Who am I? Why am I here?"

and try to ignore the flagrant display. At the same time I feel furious about witnessing this unexpected reminder of my own frustrated sexuality. Confronted with this indignity, I simultaneously envy and loathe them for their attitude, which broadcasts that they are entitled to the satisfaction of their sexual urges.

Am I not entitled?

Who am I? Why am I here? I can almost hear Buzz say, "How the fuck should I know? The only thing I know is that I'd rather be getting it on with my beautiful girlfriend than listening to an old broad like you."

Thwarted completely in my efforts to involve the rest of the class in a meaningful conversation, I finally decide that this behaviour is an insult, not only to my professional standards, but also to my personal sensibilities. The couple is happy to oblige when I ask them to leave. They walk out the door with an exaggerated air of righteousness, the pretty girl following the swaggering youth with the grace of a ballet dancer, her slim hips swaying, her long legs barely covered by a floaty little skirt. An image of their youthful bodies lingers in my mind and I'm left to stew in my own dissatisfaction.

Dissatisfaction. Disgust with the way that Brian and I have bogged down, trying to finalize our separation agreement. I've talked to him, told him that I can't enter into a trust for Sarah. Still, we continue to hover around the financial issues of our divorce like creatures circling a fire. Wary of getting too close to the flames and being burned, we are alternatively stalled or reasonable to a fault.

"The king was in his counting-house, counting out his money, the queen was in the parlour, eating bread and honey."

Brian, a lawyer and mediator, and I, a counsellor, have prided ourselves that we could negotiate these treacherous waters on our own. In my case, I've left my more-than-competent lawyer to deal with nothing but the less inflammatory details of our divorce. Yet, despite our efforts to be exemplary in the dissolution of our marriage, like all divorcing couples, we are fighting over money.

If I try to kid myself about the true effect of dragging out these proceedings, a recent dream sets me straight. In this dream, I bear witness to an inhumane scene: a cat being slowly cooked alive on a barbecue. Its feet seared to the grill and unable to move, it looks at me with eyes wild with terror.

No one can convince me that this slow drain of energy hasn't been deadly.

May 25, 1997 **Gibsons, British Columbia**

split \'split *vb* to affect as if by cleaving or forcing apart; to divide or break down; to sever relations or connections.

Over the past week, I've sensed a dark mood settling in, casting a dull pallor over my feelings like a fog obliterating the sun, or a sudden drop in barometric pressure. The ocean, as a backdrop to my gardening, and the rich colours of my surroundings (always a source of inspiration) fail to move me. Instead, I see the terrain of my existence as a yawning expanse of space, equally as flat and uneventful as the prairie landscape I left six years ago. *Is this all there is?* Below the heaviness lurks a creeping feeling of dread.

Approaching the end of May, the school year begins to wind down. Plans over the next five weeks include field trips, camp days, sports days and the final, year-end school picnic at a nearby campsite. The exuberance of these days stands in stark contrast to my feeling of ennui. *It's too soon to slow down, to slide into the languid days of summer.*

Had I been fully utilized or employed throughout the past nine months I might feel otherwise, might welcome the alfresco afternoons, the easy days filled with warm pleasures. As it is, I feel only a sense of failure. The full appreciation of my leisure eludes me.

My mood spills over into a meeting that Brian and I have set up with the school principal to discuss whether Sarah should skip grade three and go directly into grade four in the fall. As we begin our conversation, the word *skip* triggers a sense of alarm that takes me back to my own childhood.

I hear my father's angry challenge, *"Who do you think you are?"* The question, now internalized and one that I ask myself, plunges me into a frenzied emotional paralysis. My present turmoil raises the fear that I will unwittingly thrust Sarah onto the horns of the same dilemma that I've wrestled with most of my life. Are we expecting Sarah to continue the same precarious balancing act that I experienced between too smart, not smart enough; too pretty, not pretty enough; too bold, not daring enough? Treacherous and slippery, the answer to these questions depended upon the whim of an outside authority and changed from moment to moment.

As the adults discussing the idea, we finally decide to leave the decision to Sarah as to whether she wants to move ahead or remain with the same classmates she's known since preschool. I'm confident that she'll sort it out for herself over the next few days. I'm also relieved that I don't have to make the decision myself, that I only need to help her mull it over in whatever brief snatches of time we can find between breakfast and leaving for school, or between bath and bedtime.

But the impact of the issue does not end here. On the contrary, it compounds when I arrive home from walking Sarah to school. Before heading into the house, I grab my pruning shears and cut a bouquet of roses from Sarah's and my personal bushes, which we bought as gifts for each other on Mother's Day. Hers is a warm coral while mine is a clear pink. I feel a surge of appreciation for these beauties as I carry them upstairs to arrange in a vase.

I set the roses on the counter, choose the hand-blown glass vase that has been the centrepiece of my hall table since shortly after my marriage, carry it into the kitchen and fill it with water. As I set the vase back down on the counter, I hear a loud popping sound so sudden that it takes my breath away. Instantly, water is pouring over the counter, onto the floor, onto my feet. I'm suddenly holding what now looks like an extravagant dunce cap: the cone shaped top of the vase. Incredulously, I lift it up to my face and gaze through a small hard hole where the top has been severed from the base.

The vase was a extravagant purchase that I made in Calgary ten years ago on Joann's urgings, "Go for it! It's absolutely beautiful!" Since then, it has remained among my collection of favourite vases, many of which are gifts from my mother and grandmother. Less valuable in real terms, these keepsakes are precious because they remind me of the bouquets of flowers they have held over the years: lilies-of-the-valley in a creamy lustreware vase, blue and purple pansies in a stout Moorecroft vase, heavy stems of rhododendrons in a tall Waterford vase. The sudden shattering of my vase leaves me feeling vulnerable and ungrounded. I have lost my base; I am no longer intact.

I begin fretting about the incident, projecting my fears and ideas about its meaning onto Sarah.

How would she react without the security of her long-time classmates? Would this move knock her off balance? Shatter her confidence and sense of belonging? Would the other students ask, "Who does she think she is?" and turn their backs on her? And conversely, if she doesn't move, is she settling for mediocrity, just to be part of a group?

There are no easy answers. Driving to Brian's house last night for dinner, Sarah lets me know just how fed up she's become with my belabouring the subject. Turning to me, she says point-blank, "Mom, you're really irritating me. Why do you have to talk so seriously about this? It's no big deal."

She's absolutely right. I have been serious about this, almost making myself sick in the process.

"Besides," she continues, still irritated, "I've made up my mind."

"Oh," I come back brightly, "can you tell me what you have decided?"

"Yup," she replies firmly. "I've decided to stay with my class."

"Hey, that's great, Sarah! I knew you would figure it out for yourself. Congratulations! I'll let the school know what you want to do." By the time we knock on Brian's door, it's already a closed issue. Yet dinner at his house with Mary and her family proves to be a painful break of another sort. Throughout the evening, I protest to myself, *What's going on here? Why can't anything remain the same?*

I'm in for a surprise when I see how comfortably Brian has assumed his new roles, not only as Mary's partner, but also as gracious host and enthusiastic cook. Everything about this domestic scene, including his generous acceptance of Mary's family, tells me that he has shifted his loyalties completely from me to her. It is vividly clear that I have been eased into a minor role as guest and observer, while Brian and Mary have moved to the centre stage of their own lives.

Suddenly, I feel like an extra in a tightly-knit cast. Only minutes after dinner is finished, I stand up to leave, thank them, and make a quick exit. My pyrex plate, which bore my homemade lemon meringue pie, is already washed and tucked under my arm. Brian is just another body I hug briefly before starting up the long flight of stairs.

This morning, writing in my journal and waiting for

Sarah to return home after spending the night with her dad, I feel the weight of loss press heavily on my chest. I start to cry. Like water spilling over the counter from a broken vase, my tears cannot be contained or controlled.

June 27, 1997 **Gibsons, British Columbia**

dis•cov•er \dis'kə-vər *vb* to reveal; to make known or visible; to obtain sight or knowledge of for the first time.

I've had a breakthrough while mowing the lawn, which isn't as strange as it sounds. In fact, when I think of creativity, I know that my best ideas come when I'm doing something physical, when I'm not trying to figure out things in my head. Moments of inspiration arrive of their own bidding while I'm involved in seemingly mundane chores: ironing, washing windows or weeding. Once my body is engaged, my mind can cease its mental gymnastics. Dropping its agendas and hyper-vigilance, it becomes alert, yet restful; open, yet detached. My eureka moment happens during one of these times.

Backtracking a week, I'm anxiously waiting for the rain to stop so that I can go outside and mow the lawn. Finally, the weather clears up and the grass dries. I make my move. For me, mowing the lawn is always satisfying work, from the pleasure of pushing a dependable machine, to the joy of creating a grass sculpture in my own back yard.

Down, across, up and over; down, across, up and over. The recently-sharpened blade cuts neat parallel lines which, when joined, form a series of squares-within-squares of ever diminishing size. Rendered more receptive by the steady repetitive motion—*down, across, up and over*—my mind opens gracefully to reveal a greater wisdom.

In a flash of insight, I know the meaning of these past ten months. The changes, or transitions, I have been struggling with are more ancient, more inevitable, and less personal than I imagined. The landscape I have been living is one of *Initiation:* that cross-cultural rite of passage that employs ritual and ordeals (both psychological and physical) to shock the initiate into an expanded consciousness. The objective is to catapult the initiate into a deeper truth concerning his or her identity, gifts, or purpose in life. The terrors of the process are designed to burn off all but the essential self.

I suddenly understand that these desperate months mark the stage of *Initiation* called *Death*. From this archetypal perspective, I reframe the onslaught of emotional trials I have encountered, which reach back at least six years, as sacred suffering for the purpose of transformation. The language of *Initiation* captures the starkness of this stage: betrayal, loss, lack of meaning, lack of movement, emptiness, scarring, liminality. The figurative annihilation of the former self must be complete before an authentic self can emerge and assume a new place in the community. Naming the journey brings dignity to my suffering.

I know this landscape intimately. I could teach others about Initiation, about honouring themselves while they are struggling in this painful process. I know this process from the inside, out: from my writing, from the life I've been living, from my embroidery.

I feel a sudden impulse to abandon my mower, to run into the house and look at, as with new eyes, four particular works of embroidery that I now realize are replete with significance. I park my machine haphazardly across the orderly rows of fresh-cut lawn and dash inside.

Moving excitedly from one room to the next, I study each piece, marvelling that although I wasn't specifically conscious that this was *Initiation*, I was doing my inner work nonetheless. Using my threads, needles and stitches, I was making meaning of the massive changes confronting self, soul, and psyche, guided only by an intuitive need to use certain colours and specific images at a particular time. With this new understanding that I was living through an initiatory experience, the meaning stitched into each image becomes immediately evident and symbolic of a specific stage of the process.

My embroidery for Stage One, or *Separation*, uses landscape as a visual metaphor to comment on the unfamiliar setting, both geographic and psychological, that I found myself in six years ago when I had just arrived on the coast. I was wrestling with feelings of confusion and alienation.

For Stage Two, or *Purification*, I use the red and orange of fire to reflect my pain over the loss of my marriage.

Stage Three, *Death*, is marked by the image of a heart ravaged by fire; the blue blotches on the watery background suggest a primordial connection to tears and grief.

Finally, I look at my most recent work and recognize Stage Four, *New Knowledge.* A potent black flower bursts into life on a rich green field. The yellow and pink background, like the light of dawn, speaks of hope and new beginnings.

In retrospect, it's suddenly so clear. Following the map called *Initiation*, I can see that I am headed towards the final stage known as *Rebirth*.

Yet, despite my desire to arrive at this glorious conclusion of my journey, I recognize that any attempt to meddle with the natural cycle of change would be a waste of energy. Ultimately, the mystery will endure and I will continue to be governed by a will more powerful than my own. Still, understanding the immutable laws of the process in no way diminishes my enthusiasm for what I already know is important work.

As I return outside to finish my mowing, the seed of an idea to design a workshop on change, from the perspective of initiation, has taken root and is beginning to grow. My unbridled joy in this moment harkens to the abundance of blessings that is the promise of *Rebirth*.

From this launching point, I throw myself into the tasks at hand with new-found energy. For instance, I spent most of last Friday with my aunt in Vancouver, mainly to meet with her accountant in order to determine whether to formalize a complaint with the British Columbia Law Society over a problem with her lawyer. Up at 5:30 to catch the 6:20 ferry, it's too early to dress for the day in anything but jeans and a shirt. But knowing that I'll meet Colin for dinner later at a beautiful waterfront restaurant, I bring along my new Ralph Lauren outfit.

My aunt and I meet with her accountant in his cubby-hole office, in a concrete-block building. His long grey toupee is combed carefully up and over the crown of his head and he's obviously wearing a new yellow silk tie. He seems indifferent to his surroundings but interested in his appearance.

"That's a beautiful tie you're wearing." I remark.

"Thank you," he beams, "it's a Donna Karan."

The vivid yellow tie lights up the drab office like a daffodil on a dull morning. It is refreshing and at the same time, slightly startling.

Despite his tendency to digress, he's a decent fellow. With his help, we resolve the question of whether there is sufficient evidence of misuse of trust funds to support a claim. He navigates us skillfully through the murky waters surrounding the issue and brings us to the safe solid shore of much-needed clarity. Ultimately, the matter boils down to who would be believed. An elderly woman or a lawyer? We are all certain that there has been blatant wrongdoing, yet the consensus at the end of the meeting is that this territory would be too slippery to embark upon with any degree of confidence.

We leave the office three hours later, not with the answer we had hoped for, but with an answer nonetheless. We dart from the building into the drizzly day and make a dash to the car. Once inside the car, my aunt seems almost upbeat. If nothing else, the meeting has allowed her to tell the complete story of her troubles, which has brought relief and closure.

We spend the afternoon running errands and arrive back at her apartment in time for a late cup of tea. With it, we share the pleasure of homemade cookies and the satisfaction of knowing that she's completed a difficult chapter in her life.

Suddenly I notice the time. I make a quick change into my new outfit, kiss her good bye, and leave the apartment feeling excited and worldly. Looking for the road to the restaurant and fighting rush-hour traffic, I overshoot the turnoff by blocks before realizing my error and turning back. When I finally join Colin at the restaurant, I'm an hour late.

Unlike the accountant's office, the restaurant is exquisite, the setting inspiring. Colin is seated at a window table overlooking the sea walk and English Bay when the maitre'd seats me across from him. We exchange greetings. Colin smiles at me warmly and is quick to ask, "What would you like to drink?"

Noticing that he already has a glass of wine, I reply without hesitation, "I would love a glass of champagne."

"Do you serve champagne by the glass?" Colin asks the maitre'd.

"Of course," comes back the reply, and then speaking to me directly, "I'll bring you a glass of Domaine Chandon."

Dinner is a fabulous affair. I feast on the flavours as well as the sumptuous colours of the decor. The smooth crisp drink, the mouth-watering Arctic char stuffed with shrimp, the butter yellow and apricot walls, the rich blue trim and burgundy-black rosewood detailing. Throughout the meal I'm almost euphoric, *not* from the champagne, but from the pleasures and beauty flooding my senses. When I raise my glass to acknowledge the moment we're sharing, I am toasting life, companionship, and the dramatic changes I'm beginning to feel. Like seismic shifts registering deep within the earth's crust, the shifts within my being will trigger bold reverberations in my outer life.

The impact continues into this morning when I send Sarah off with her father for a two-week visit to Alberta. Knowing that she's in safe hands and that for the time being I'm relieved of childcare duties, I pour myself a cup of coffee and sit down on the sofa in the garden room to contemplate my immediate future. An idea presents itself in a matter of minutes. *Why not see if Colin wants to join us—Joann, her partner, Frank, and me—when we go boating over the long weekend in July?*

Tracking him down on his cell phone is not difficult.

He picks up the phone and I identify myself. Grabbing a quick breath of resolve, I dive in directly, "Colin, Sarah's just left with her dad for the ferry and finally some space has opened up around me. I'm wondering whether you'd like to go boating with us next weekend? Frank's taking his boat and he's talking about sailing to Saltspring Island. You could bring your boat to meet us."

There's a pause and then a perfectly reasonable question, "Who will you be travelling with?" he asks.

"Well," I offer, "I'll go with you."

Neat and simple, my answer reveals that I've moved from ambivalence and self-doubt to decisive action.

July 4, 1997 Saltspring Island, British Columbia

cel•e•brate\'se-la-ˌbrāt *vb* to observe a holiday by festivities; to perform a sacrament publicly and with appropriate rites.

A week later, Colin and I leave on our boating trip. I finish loading the cart with our provisions, laughing when I see what we've packed: clothes to cover any weather condition and enough food for twice as many people. The cart heaped high, I push it carefully *bump, bump, bump* down the gangplank, along the wharf, and park it next to Colin's cabin cruiser, *Santana*.

He looks up when he hears me arrive, smiles and says, "If you can set things up inside, I'll continue getting the boat ready."

"Sure," I reply easily. I start unloading the cart and carrying bags and boxes down into the cabin. Seeing the interior of the boat for the first time, I admire the sleek compactness that feels like a luxury hotel suite. Every convenience is at our fingertips; beautiful design matches space with utility.

I quickly assess *what goes where* and start putting things away. Food into the galley fridge, beer and wine and *ooh, this is a nice bottle of champagne*, into the cockpit fridge above. *Which reminds me, today is the fourth of July, Independence Day*. Next I take a pile of thick turquoise towels, place some of them in the head and stack the rest of them on one of the narrow berths in aft cabin. I hang clothes in a slim compartment, place Colin's bag in one cupboard, mine in another, and leave my sunglasses and books on a ledge above the table.

Being invited onto Colin's boat, it's as if I've been handed a snapshot of the man. Noticing that he has already made up the big front berth with beautiful fresh linens, I know that he cares about comfort and pleasure. The bedding is as inviting as the towels are plush and thick. *This is a meticulous man. There is nothing random about his world.*

Once everything is stowed safely below, I climb up the stairs to the cockpit and join Colin as he prepares to back the boat away from the dock. I slide along the white leather bench to sit next to him. "What else can I do to help?" I ask.

"You can get ready to pull up the fenders when we've cleared the dock. Then you can store them in the big bin on the deck."

He stops talking and begins to manoeuvre the boat skillfully out of the marina and south into the Straight of Georgia.

"When did you begin boating?"I ask.

"I grew up on the water," he replies simply. "From the time my brother and I were kids, we were out in boats ... diving, fishing, exploring. Mainly around this area or in the Gulf Islands. There's nothing I like better than being on the water."

"Well, you obviously know what you're doing. And this is a completely new world for me. It's fabulous being here with you, watching you."

I realize that what I've just said is the absolute truth. I'm a happy woman sitting next to him, my arm resting along the back of the bench (I can touch his shoulder if I want to) and my bare legs stretched out in front of me.

A sudden imperious voice cuts through my thoughts, *"Look at you in those shorts."* Immediately, I recognize the uninvited guest as Athena, goddess of beauty and upholder of standards.

"You should be ashamed of yourself, wearing shorts with unsightly legs".

"Hey, wait a minute," I snap back, *"I've actually given this a lot of thought. My decision to wear shorts was more important than wondering what to wear. The way I looked at it, there wasn't really an alternative. Either I was going to start living or crawl back into a hole and die."*

"Oh, don't be so dramatic," she spits.

"Well, what do you expect me to wear?"

"Something more appropriate."

"I had to decide whether to leap back into the land of the living or slink away in shame, hiding my imperfections and giving up any hope of rejoining the human race. That's what it came down to."

"Suit yourself. See if I care." She exits in disgust.

"Good riddance," I mutter to myself and pull my attention back to the glorious afternoon and the trip across the open waters.

Colin maintains the boat at a steady cruising speed of fifteen knots. The trip takes just over two hours. Slowing down at our rendezvous point and the entrance to Ganges Harbour, we spot the sailboat we're looking for. Frank's boat, *Libelle,* drifts nearby with its sails down. Frank hears the sound of our approach, appears on the deck and waves a greeting.

We establishes a safe, yet sociable, distance between the two boats and kill the engine of *Santana*. The day becomes calm. The boat rolls gently. The only sounds are voices floating faintly over the water and seagulls squawking as they look for food.

Colin shows me how to use the winch to lower the inflatable dinghy into the water. Within minutes, we've rowed over to the sailboat and are climbing up the rope ladder and onto the deck. Laughter and goodwill, handshakes and hugs abound. We are now a party of six: Frank and Joann, Colin and I and a couple from Portland. A lazy afternoon awaits us. The only pressing questions are: "Who needs sunscreen? Is everyone comfortable? Who wants a drink? Who wants to go swimming?"

I light up immediately at the idea of jumping into the ocean. Without stopping to ask about the temperature (which I find out later is a mere 56 degrees), I lower myself down the ladder and drop into the water. The shock is instantaneous and stunning. I gasp for breath. A band of steel grabs the back of my neck like a vice. My body flails in panic.

Like the sacrament of baptism, my brief plunge into the frigid water is less about swimming than about ceremony. Nothing further is required of me. Within seconds, I am clambering madly back up the ladder and yelling out to the others who are hanging over the edge of the boat, watching me with admiration, "Well, at least I've done it!"

They acknowledge my symbolic immersion with hearty congratulations and accept me back into the tribe on deck. Colin stands nearby, waiting to wrap me in an oversized, warmed-by-the-sun towel. Standing there like a kid, teeth rattling, lips blue and shaking uncontrollably, I welcome his efforts to revive me, rough as they are. Finally, clenching the towel tightly around my body, I huddle on the deck, surrounded by a tight clutch of friends, waiting for the sun to minister its healing warmth.

Colin is watching me closely. "Why don't we row back to the boat so you can take a hot shower?"

"You mean you've got a shower on your boat?" I ask incredulously.

"Yes, I do. And I think that's what you need."

I don't need convincing.

Within minutes, I'm standing on the swim grid at the back of his boat. He holds the shower hose above my head and lets the hot soothing water pour over me. Washed with pleasure, my body begins to relax. My soul softens in this exquisite moment. I feel like a queen.

He leaves me to finish up and disappears downstairs. A few moments later he returns holding two glasses of champagne. He smiles and hands me one, "Here's to today!" he toasts, "to you and me ... out here on the water. To good times!" We hold each other's gaze as we take a sip.

By the time I change into dry, clean clothes, it's time for dinner. We leave what's left of the champagne for a night cap and place the bottle back in the fridge, deciding quickly what food we will take to the sailboat for our communal feast.

When dinner is over, everyone is satisfied and sleepy. The party winds down. For the second time today, we row back to Colin's boat in the dinghy. He rigs it up on the winch while I step down into the galley to pour us the last of the champagne. When he appears I hand him his glass and say appreciatively, "Thank you, Colin, for a wonderful day."

"You're welcome," he replies warmly. "I hope we have many more."

He finishes his drink, sets it down, and moves towards the fore cabin. "Would you like to join me upfront?" he asks, indicating the big V-berth.

I know the difference between a king's bed and a nun's bed. The choice is easy.

"Yes," I smile. "I'd love to."

July 8, 1997 **Gibsons, British Columbia**

plunge \'plənj *vb* to throw or cast oneself, as if into water; enter quickly into something.

This morning I wake up leisurely in my own bed.It is two days after our boating trip and the day after I finish dealing with the deluge that followed immediately after my return. The snippet of a dream wafts at the edge of my consciousness. My deceased grandmother, appearing as she did thirty years ago, sits quietly in her favourite chair, looking out at me. Without words but with her imposing presence, she conveys a silent comment that I don't understand. Then four or five filmy figures slip into the scene with her. They hover around her chair, motionless and mute. I scream when I see them. Everyone, including my grandmother, fades and disappears.

Although I'm not surprised that she would have something to say about my weekend with Colin, her message is as shadowy and insubstantial as the filmy figures. Still, this morning I find my reflections about the past five days more interesting than thoughts about the meaning of a phantom visit. I'm content to curl up like a pampered cat. *Besides, there's no reason to get up. And it seems to have stopped raining. I might as well enjoy my solitude while Sarah is still away. Take the time,* I urge myself, *to savour recent events.*

Over the three days that we spend on the water, the weather remains constant: hot and clear. But the following morning, I wake up at home to an entirely different world. It's pouring, literally buckets. Trying to salvage the poor plants in the garden under the front porch, I place two, twenty-gallon garbage buckets under the eaves to catch the water that is spilling over the clogged troughs. With no alternative run-off, the water pours down relentlessly onto the flowers below. My impatiens take the worst beating. It seems that their struggle over the past six weeks to gain a flowery foothold in the meagre root-entangled soil may be in vain.

In theory, my plan for water removal is a good one; in fact, it poses a problem. Once the buckets are full of water, I find that they're too heavy to haul away and dump elsewhere. Thinking fast and working even faster, I revise my plan and start bailing out the bigger buckets with a smaller pail, getting rid of the water by flinging it away from the garden in great flying sheets. Plants unfortunate enough to be within striking distance are hit broadside. Throughout most of yesterday I struggle to stay ahead of the rain, yet in some ways, my Samaritan efforts serve another important purpose.

Instead of being swamped by emotion when I start thinking about my weekend with Colin, I tend to my plants that are at risk of death by drowning. Figuratively, I try to get my land legs back under me after spending three days on the water. I need time to process certain new information that is both wonderful and startling.

I have been with a man. I have made love with a man. I have touched and been touched by a man. The reality of this experience seeps slowly into my being. Something fundamental has shifted in the core of me.

Later in the day, I meet Joann at her house. I haven't seen her since she and Frank set sail from Saltspring Island, leaving Colin and me to spend a few final hours exploring the beaches around the harbour. Joann takes a stool at her kitchen counter. I settle into the same old chair that my grandmother sat in, in this morning's dream. Joann smiles brightly and launches into the topic at hand, "So ... how was your weekend?"

I enter these waters carefully, resisting the temptation to categorize too quickly or too casually.

"Well, ... it was ... fabulous," feeling the inadequacy of words.

How do I describe the sensory impressions still floating in my consciousness like petals of flowers dancing on drafts of air, or solitary music notes? My impulse is to simply let them be, without trying to muddy them with meaning. Too soon, too private, too precious to organize into tidy compartments. I end up saying very little.

But when I return home after our visit, I make a quick telephone call back to Saltspring Island. I reach the same woman whom Colin and I met selling sensuous body products at the outdoor market and order a bottle of the massage oil that was our favourite when we smelled the samples on the weekend. Continuing to steer clear of analyzing my moves, I let the gesture speak for itself.

July 26, 1997 **Gibsons, British Columbia**

stroke \'**strōk**\ *vb* to set the pace as in swimming or rowing a boat; to pass the hand repeatedly in the same direction.

Weekends at my work site have taken on an entirely new meaning. Whereas once I drove to the project on Saturday, worked, went home, and returned on Sunday to complete my two-day stint, now I meet Colin at his home on Friday afternoon and spend the weekend with him. Except for the blocks of time between noon and 4:00, when I'm dressed for business and introducing customers to the project, we're either catching an early morning walk on the beach, collecting shells, puttering in his garden, or riding bikes along the power line trail above his home.

My world opens up wondrously as he shares his knowledge of nature with me. Although I have been showing customers this site for ten months, describing the wilderness preserve, the walking paths and moorage for boats, it is only now that it comes alive for me. My eyes sharpen to spy an eagle perched on a craggy tree, detect the difference between a mallard or merganser duck, pick out a sea lion basking in the sun on an outcropping of rock, or recognize the telltale signs that sea otters have visited the dock. The list of birds that I've sighted and recorded in a new birdwatcher's journal grows steadily: cormorant, blue heron, osprey, oystercatcher, killdeer, sandpiper, plover.

After I lock the sales office, I'm back at his condominium within sixty seconds. Before long, I've changed, grabbed a quick cup of tea, which he has waiting for me, and am ready for our next venture. Frequently, I pull on my bathing suit and dive into the ocean for a swim, feeling especially delighted when the day has been hot enough to warm up the water. But the temperature has become incidental. It's now a point of personal pride to *just do it*—swim—regardless of how it feels. The more days I spend with Colin embracing his active lifestyle, the more I recall my younger athletic self, the more I discover my love of the ocean and all things wild and natural. I feel as if I've been released from solitary confinement.

This afternoon I forego my swim because we've invited friends for cocktails and dinner. They arrive early in order to sit outside and enjoy the still-glorious afternoon. Colin has prepared his favourite summer drink of cranberry juice and black currant vodka. A large jug chills in the fridge. He pours each of us a generous drink, which we accept gratefully before heading outside to the south-facing patio.

The drinks, the smoked salmon, the company of great friends. This is perfection. I marvel aloud, "This is as good at it gets. Right here. Right now."

Suddenly, I need to express my joy in a different way and run inside to find a story which I've written recently. "OK, folks," I announce as I return, holding up two sheets of paper, "I've got something to read to you." They indulge me with easy humour.

"Come over here," I beckon to Colin who is standing by the door. "This is for you as much as anyone."

He comes to my side, lays a hand on my shoulder, and I begin, "This one's called *Suit Yourself.*"

Where I grew up in northern British Columbia, our only lake was glacier-fed and ice-cold. Being a family of non-swimmers, we visited the lake no more than once or twice a year. On those rare excursions, my mother was designated driver and swimming teacher.

Despite her deep aversion to water, her sense of duty required that she demonstrate for us, swimming as she did, like a turtle, her head held high and stiff above the water. Following her lead, my sister and I adopted her cautious style. Still, I was troubled by two equally unattractive choices: either swim out and over my head and risk drowning, or stay in closer to shore with my feet sinking into gooey mud and slimy seaweeds brushing my legs.

After each expedition, my mother placed a large tin basin on the washstand in the back porch and directed Joann and me to practise putting our faces in the water. In-out, in-out, I cranked my face from side to side as the old tom cat rubbed against my legs, reassuring me that this, too, would pass.

After I left home and the glacier-fed lake, my swimming was more cosmetic than functional. Mainly, I graced a deck chair by the side of a pool. All was well for thirtysomething years until my sister and I acquired a waterfront property. Shortly thereafter, I began to get wind of what was tantamount to family heresy: curious whispers about Joann swimming in the ocean. As reports filtered back to me, I felt a certain envy in response to her audacity. Finally, I was compelled to join her in the ocean, which was no less freezing than our childhood lake. Gradually something happened. I realized that I loved these outings.

As of this summer my swimming feats include plunging from a boat into 56 degree water off the coast of Saltspring Island, a midnight swim, sans suit, in Pender Harbour Lake, swims from deserted beaches, public beaches—here, there, everywhere. I've stashed bathing suits in various homes and cottages along the coastline like Hansel and Gretel's crumbs, should I get a sudden urge to leap into the brine. My thirst has become unquenchable. A new friend (I reach up to touch Colin's hand resting on my shoulder) notes my growing passion for le sport and surprises me one day with my first Speedo goggles. Handing me a flashy pink and blue pair, he remarks, "These will help you put your face in the water." And as a second thought, "You'll be a great swimmer—you've got long legs."

Hearing his comments, my joy becomes unbounded; my aquatic ambition grows as large as the ocean. As a symbolic gesture to mark my 50th birthday, I have declared that I will enter the one-mile swim from Gibsons to Keats Island next summer. I can see it already. I'll buy myself a red tank suit like the one I wore years ago and emerge from the ocean, triumphant and shining, like an initiate completing a watery rite of passage.

I'm proud to say that I have dispensed with the outmoded story about being a non-swimmer with the same ease that I would dispose of an old bathing suit. Now that I'm a swimmer, I'm free to wear whatever suits my fancy.

I conclude with a laugh, pause briefly and then turn to Colin. "So here's to you," I say, raising my crantini glass, "for your part in the emergence of a new me!"

"Here's to Colin," the others respond with noisy cheer.

"Speaking of Colin," someone shouts, "what's happening with dinner?"

That's our cue to get the food on the table. Throughout dinner, the sky is a brilliant show of light. The soft pink wash of early evening turns into a blazing backdrop of orange and gold. When the sun sinks and drops into the ocean, this is the signal that our evening is drawing to a close.

Colin and I see our friends to the front door, say goodnight, and turn eagerly towards each other. On a sudden impulse, he says, "Let's take the canoe out past the breakwater before it gets completely dark. There's a small beach just around the corner."

Wasting no time, we pull on our bathing suits, grab towels, haul the canoe down to the beach, and launch it. We paddle together with an easy rhythm and the sleek red craft slips through the water. Ten minutes later, we pull into shore, lift the canoe carefully onto the rocks, and lay down our towels.

Suddenly, we know why we're here. We answer our unspoken question, *Do we dare?* and begin peeling off our bathing suits.

Moonlight splashes on his shoulders. A slim band of lights runs along the distant horizon and he lowers his body towards mine. I reach up to meet him.

Like the worn-out suit in my story, our bathing suits are tossed aside. No longer needed, they lie discarded on the rocks.

Stone Drawings

In my dream I am standing in my backyard behind a guardrail that overlooks a deep hole. Around my feet are several large rocks. I see no value in them and begin to throw them into the hole. It is deeper than I imagined and, like a well-shaft, it may also have water at the bottom. As I throw one rock over the guardrail I notice that it bears a hieroglyphic: the outline of an angel. On a second rock I see the outline of a foot, which suggests an Egyptian shoe or sole.

Although I initially discount these rocks as worthless, I now understand that the drawings make them invaluable. The rocks bear messages from the realm of archetype and spirit.

August 2, 1997 **Gibsons, British Columbia**

fan \'fan *vb* to blow or breathe upon to kindle a flame; stir up activity; to stimulate.

Tonight Colin and I are going to the anniversary party of old friends from Calgary—Charles and Margaret. For me, being invited to their home is fun and familiar. It is the wonderful waterfront property where Brian, Sarah and I lived for three months in the spring of 1991, before taking the plunge and moving from the prairie in the fall of the same year. During our idyllic stay and after we moved to the coast, we spent many hours together, their family and ours, hiking up the knoll behind their home with its spectacular view of the town below, wandering along the beach in front of their property, eating al fresco on their front deck or in the dining room with its generous views of Howe Sound.

For Colin, however, going to their home is another matter. This is a hot August night, yet he arrives cold, knowing no one but me. Furthermore, I have danced with this crowd before, both literally and figuratively, although not specifically with Charles. However, I am familiar with the repartee required to pull off the evening with aplomb.Colin has none of these same advantages.

The home's furnishings reflect the easy elegance of the owners. Among them are chintz sofas and chairs, hand-carved wooden artifacts whittled by a retired neurosurgeon during his frequent visits, books collected from the Writers' Festival over the years, and vases of fresh flowers. During my time at this home, I name it the Gourmet Cottage, which refers to the scrumptious food the owners serve when they are on the coast and the unobstructed ocean, island and mountain views.

Tonight's party, a celebration of thirty years of married life for Charles and Margaret, is a celebration for myself as well, marking thirty days, plus or minus, that I've been with a new man. As a link between my former and present life, I'm anxious to introduce these long-time friends to Colin and openly declare my renewed coupled status. In many ways, I've come home.

Like a woman and a man, the gracious home and rugged setting are a study in contrasts. Elements that evoke the gentle charm of a country cottage nudge up directly against the bold beauty of massive boulders, creosote logs, broken shells, bird droppings and lank seaweed. My senses explode with this heady mix of sights, smells, and sounds: the weathered shake roof and the clumps of moss clinging to it; the sage green cottage with its fresh cream trim; the flower beds running in boisterous colour alongside a white picket fence; the laurel hedge, resistant to all efforts to stem its glorious growth; the smell of fresh-cut wood stacked against the outside wall.

The fragrance of roses and honeysuckle lingers in my memory even as it is absorbed into the heavy salt air. The ocean pounds relentlessly against the shore, suggesting things unspoken, untamed.

Colin and I arrive at the party in time for cocktails. As we walk towards the crowd of people mingling on the lawn,

I notice our host. Standing behind a make-shift bar set up outdoors, he presides over the event with the ease of a king holding court. We step up to the bar. Colin stands slightly behind me.

Charles' opening remark, "Aaaah, darling, aren't you looking gorgeous tonight!" confirms my feelings of relief when I studied myself in the full-length mirror in my bedroom an hour earlier. His eyes sweep over my tanned face and arms and down my body. Appraising the silk skirt, the form-fitting black jersey top, the gold necklace and earrings, he assures me, without, words, that I am desirable. We exchange a few comments. I introduce Colin.

"Ah, yes, the task at hand," Charles remarks, pulling himself back to what he's doing. He gestures with his arm towards the wide array of liquor and mixes on the bar and asks with an exaggerated air, "A Marguerita for the lady?"

Laughing at his antics and quickly confirming that Colin wants the same drink, I nod. Charles, having assumed this would be our drink of choice, is already attending to the blender. In a single streamlined gesture, he checks the lid on the glass mixing jug, flips the control button to High, blends the drink, lifts the lid, raises the jug triumphantly over his head, reaches for a gold plastic party tumbler, pours the cool green drink into the gold tumbler in mid air in front of my face and with a flourish, hands me my cocktail.

Through this brief encounter, Colin, more inclined towards action than words, seems to shrink and recoil as Charles' six-foot-four frame expands exponentially, revelling in his own largesse. After an hour of mingling on the lawn, we're urged to drink up and move inside.

Served against a background of our host's favourite 60's music, dinner is a deliciously raucous affair with fresh salmon marinated in herbs and barbecued on an outside grill, a bounty of steamed organic vegetables from the local market gardener, and California fume blancs and French beaujolais. Having already piqued our pleasure with drinks and food, Charles stands up to announce the next item on the bill of fare, issuing a challenge to all party-goers to compose a limerick for their wedding anniversary.

Immediately, happy mayhem ensues with groans from those guests either uncomfortable with writing in general or the literary form in particular, indifference from those more interested in savouring dessert and after-dinner drinks, and enthusiasm from those of us eager to rise to the literary occasion. Within a few minutes, I, too, am up on my feet, toasting the couple with my own clever rhyme, using my words to strike the fine literary line between overly cautious good form and blatantly bad taste. The rousing response to my poem informs me that others appreciate my verbal acuity. Colin, however, remains quiet.

Good humour abounds and the evening progresses with increased intensity. The music is suddenly louder. Heightened energy pulsates among the guests and we are asked to move along to the next venue, dancing outside on the deck.

The moon hangs high in the sky, its cool light flooding across the ocean and onto the assembled guests. Tall lumieres light the four corners of the deck. Citronella candles placed on small patio tables do double duty by keeping the bugs at bay and adding a lemon-fresh scent to the air. The night takes on a magical glow; the setting becomes more seductive in the encroaching darkness. In the flickering light from the open-pit fire on the beach just below the deck, women become more alluring, men more dashing. Music is piped out from the living room to the deck. Couples dance.

Colin and I move outside and stand for a minute at the side of the deck, digesting the events of the evening. Suddenly, Charles is standing in front of me. Without acknowledging Colin who is already slipping into the peripheries of my awareness and out of view, Charles grabs my hand, "Let's have that dance." He leads me smoothly around several couples to find a place to dance on the wooden deck.

I have assumed that Charles' height would translate into disjointed dancing so I'm surprised that dancing with him is more satisfying than I expected. He holds me close against his tall frame, moving confidently. "I've always liked a man who dances with authority," I remark, appreciating his boldness and teasing him at the same time. One dance dissolves into another, into another, into another. The king in his court dances with whomever he pleases and I, as if wearing the red shoes from the fairy tale of the same name, am unable to stop my feet from moving.

In the blur of faces as we weave and turn, I am uncertain whether Colin has just approached me to ask for a dance or whether I am imagining this. In either event, I continue dancing with Charles until I hear Colin's voice coming from a darkened distance, "I'm getting the hell out of here." The chill in his voice cuts through my mind's warm oblivion like the clock striking midnight at Cinderella's ball.

1 - 2 - 3. Startled, I bid abrupt goodbyes. Turn quickly from Charles. Slip unnoticed past the dancing couples. *4 - 5 - 6.* Dash down the stairs to the lawn. Bend over to take off my high strappy sandals. Flee across the dew-dampened lawn. *7 - 8 - 9.* Run from the glittering party and into the night towards Colin's car, which I hear pulling away on the gravel driveway. *10 - 11 - 12.*

Midnight and the party's over.

August 3, 1997 **Gibsons, British Columbia**

dis•tort \di-'sto̊rt *vb* to twist out of a normal or natural shape; to twist out of the true meaning or proportion.

The phone jolts me awake. It's Colin. His voice flat with anger, he asks in a plaintive tone, "So why did you do it?"

I feel myself sinking. I slide deeper into my down quilt and clutch it instinctively around my body for protection.

"Do we have to go into this so early?" I try to reason.

He mows me down. "I want to know why you did it." The same tone, more forceful.

Oh, my god, I groan inwardly, *he's asking for a definitive answer, one that will put his pain to bed, here and now.*

At the same time, I know that the answer is too complex to deliver in simple, black and white terms, know that it's naive to imagine that any of us ever gets to the bottom of an issue to say with certainty, "This is the reason."

I can't satisfy his demand for a clear-cut answer. Bargaining for time, I'm swamped by a tidal wave of possible replies pressing down on me: some truths, some only guessed at, some existing in a cellular memory, and others pure fantasy.

Mentally, I sift through the ideas jostling for attention, resisting the urge to be snide or superior, holding back the deluge that I imagine will only incite him further ...

Because, I reply, speaking silently to myself, *last night I remembered I was beautiful, after spending four fabulous weeks with you on the water, in your boat, slipping in and out of secret coves, anchoring at dusk; because I forgot that you were the reason I was feeling so wonderful; because I was ecstatic to be sexual and erotic again, to be touched, to feel my senses awakened, to know pleasure again; because I'm premenstrual; because when I dressed last night, I imagined I was an hierodule in the temple of Aphrodite; because in that moment I knew that I embodied beauty and sacred sexuality and that the service I performed was honourable and valued; because of shared experiences with these people from an earlier time in my life; because I was laughing and for a brief shining moment, I was a queen; because I love dancing; because I was aroused and alive; because the smell of coupling was in the air; because I had returned from the dead.*

Instead, I settle for an abridged answer and reply aloud as honestly as I can, "Maybe I fell into an old pattern, forgot I wasn't thirty any more, and that I didn't have to be dazzling like the women in our family were expected to be. Dazzling but always untouchable; nothing intended, just a show of my charm and power. All of which I mistakenly assumed would broadcast to you, 'Look at this desirable woman.'

"Isn't that what a man wants? To know that his woman is desired by other men? Doesn't that add to his measure of esteem, knowing this?"

"That disgusts me," he replies, "you're no better than a whore."

"But I didn't do anything," I protest, incredulous at this sudden vicious turn.

"You might as well have fucked him on the floor in front of everyone."

He hasn't heard me. His remark flows through a filter of his own pain.

"What did I do wrong?" he continues. "Wasn't I treating you well enough? Wasn't I telling you often enough that you're beautiful? Wasn't I fucking you enough? Obviously, I was doing something wrong."

"This wasn't about you." I try to explain. "It was about me."

"Don't give me that bullshit." The phone goes dead.

Throughout the day I wrestle to make sense of what seems to be an over-heated response to last night's incident. The depth of Colin's outrage makes me suspect that there are deeper issues than he might like to believe. I think back to my counselling training, which tells me that considering the *source* of the upset would be more helpful than arguing about *why* it happened. I know the book I need: *The Intimate Couple* by Rosenberg and Kitaen-Morse. My answer appears in *Chapter Fifteen: Fragmentation or Intermittent Insanity*. I read the following passage:

> *A common but often tragic misconception is that the things people say or do in this state of "intermittent insanity" are the truth. This is not correct. When a person is fragmented, his or her utterances and actions are clouded, warped, and exaggerated. The symptoms of fragmentation are an expression of childhood injuries repeated in a current situation.*

This brief description confirms my hunch. Curious now as to how certain elements of an old (and probably long-forgotten) incident might be replicated in last night's incident, I want to discuss this idea with Colin. I pick up the phone to call him.

The phone rings. He replies with a curt hello. He knows it's me by the number appearing on his phone display.

"Colin," I begin quietly, "I've been trying to figure out what's happening here ... trying to put two and two together. I've got an idea."

I hear a grudging, "Uh hmmm," but at least he's prepared to listen.

"You've told me a bit about your father and how he loved to entertain so lavishly. The way you describe him, six-foot-six, big and bold, holding forth in his home and enjoying himself immensely, he sounds pretty formidable. When you were a kid, your dad ... everyone and everything ... must have seemed bigger than life."

No comment. I decide to continue.

"I'm wondering if somehow the whole scene with Charles last night triggered a memory of something that happened when you were young? Something you might have forgotten that caused shame or pain?" I pause and let my words hang in the air.

Dead silence.

"What the hell are you talking about?" Cold flat anger again. "This has nothing to do with my father. And it's got nothing to do with me. I think you'd better have a closer look at yourself."

"I'm sorry I've offended you," I inhale deeply. "I'm just trying to understand. And about last night, I'm sorry I caused you so much pain. That would never be my intention."

By now, and by tacit agreement, it's clear that we need to drop the subject. We beat a hasty retreat off the phone.

As if in the aftermath of a seismic tremor, the ground upon which Colin and I have been standing has shifted.

August 10 to August 13, 1997 | **Strait of Georgia West Coast of British Columbia**

quick•en \\'kwi-kən *vb* to shine more brightly; to enter into a phase of active growth; to stimulate, revive.

Despite the rift that opened between Colin and me the night of the anniversary party, the anticipation of still more days and nights together on the boat exerts its own seductive pull. We follow through with our plans for a four-day visit to Jervis Inlet.

Shortly after I arrive at Colin's condominium, the boat is packed with provisions and our gear is stored away in the designated compartments. Colin is making last-minute adjustments to the engine. Once I'm finished below, I rejoin him in the cockpit and claim what is now my place next to him on the bench. He begins to steer the boat away from the dock and our trip begins. Unlike the boat, which is easing out of the marina at the posted *Dead Slow* speed, I'm already on full throttle. Delighted to leave behind what has been an arid existence for too long, delighted to embark upon a shimmery world of watery pleasures.

Travelling away from the coastal communities towards increasingly remote landscapes, the boat is, at once, a luxurious means of transportation and a vessel for exploring intimacy. We are now beyond the usual constraints of time and space and free to wonder, *Who is this man? Who is this woman?* Sitting beside him and watching him handle the boat with obvious expertise, I admire his understated quiet confidence and feel a strong attraction towards him. The needle of my psychic compass points to him as a powerful man and I trust this inner compass. It works with the same precision as the compass on the instrument panel of the boat.

Surrounded by water, islands, evergreens, rocks, wildlife and birds, and in the company of a man who arouses me, I'm like a famished woman who is finally fed. *I want more. More colour, texture, touch, expression. My body longs to stretch and grow. My soul longs to sing.* Suddenly, I'm starved for words as well, eager to catch an inflection or gesture and capture it on paper.

I dash downstairs to rummage through a bag and grab a pencil and spiral notebook, then return to my seat next to Colin and begin to write. My HB pencil slashes words across the page in bold uncensored thoughts as my joy simultaneously flows over the page. An idea pops into my mind. I will create a collection of poems for his Christmas gift called *Summer of Many Pleasures.* I hope this gift will express my gratitude to him for taking me to the untamed places within nature and within myself.

My God, I wonder, *how did I ever manage to suppress my appetite for sensuous pleasures?*

"That was the only way to survive the drought," comes back the wry comment.

Vividly aware of my well-being in this moment, I suddenly remember an issue that has left me feeling vaguely disquieted. While not wanting to squelch the mood of the day, I still want resolution and turn to him and ask, "Do you want to talk about what happened at the party?"

Sensing that this could plunge us into treacherous waters, he' s quick with his response. "No," he replies firmly, "let's just enjoy ourselves." His focus remains fixed on navigating the boat across the water and not diving for deeper meaning.

For me, the day on the boat with Colin is intensely erotic. The boating chart, with its blue lines and black print on a tan background, becomes provocative and richly symbolic. The names, Prince of Wales Reach and Princess Louisa Inlet, and the passage connecting the two bodies of water, suggest the magnetic pull of a man to a woman. Colin studies the chart in front of him before attempting to approach the narrow opening to Princess Louisa, before steering the sleek craft skillfully through the rapids, which could prevent access to the vast watery cave beyond. As the boat motors through the channel to finally rest at the farthest reach of the inlet, I imagine this symbolically as the masculine archetype moving towards the feminine. My own response to this man is the inevitable opening of the woman.

Suddenly, we're approaching the dock and *this man* needs my help on board. "Get ready to throw out the fenders and grab the ropes when I throw them down to you." My musing comes to an abrupt end. By the time I climb down from the boat and step onto the solid wooden dock, I've returned to the world of objects and action. Dinghy, oars, bathing suits, towels.

There's still time for a late afternoon swim. We throw our gear into the dinghy and slip away from the dock and other boats moored at the foot of Chatterbox Falls. We disappear around an outcropping of rocky shoreline, abandon our craft and jump overboard. The ocean, like tepid bath water, becomes our private playground. An hour later, we haul our satisfied bodies out of the water, heave ourselves over the inflated sides of the dinghy and flop noisily onto the bottom. Laughing together, we paddle the dinghy back to the boat for a glass of chilled chardonnay, which sounds more inviting by the moment. Colin lights the barbecue and we wait impatiently for it to heat up sufficiently to start dinner.

A chef in khaki shorts with a grin on his face and tongs in his hands, he watches over the jumbo prawns cooking on the grill. He turns to ask, "Do you know how to tell when they're cooked?"

"No, I don't," I reply, interested in this tidbit of information. "How can you tell?"

"It's when the tails curl up. That's when they're done."

I laugh at his comment and at the same time, feel proud to discover his competency in yet another arena—that of cooking. Stretched out on a leather bench in the stern's open deck and marvelling at the glorious scenery, I watch my lover prepare dinner. Cleopatra on her barge could not have felt happier. Formidable rock walls rise up sharply from the ocean, obliterating the sinking sun and the last of daylight. After dinner, darkness descends quickly. On a deliciously wicked impulse, we decide to sleep outside on the back deck in zipped-together sleeping bags. While fellow boaters wander up and down the dock no more than ten feet from where we lie, we slide deep into the covers and make love.

The next morning I awaken slowly. With my eyes still shut, I hear the sounds of a guy in a galley: *glug, glug, glug* water pours from an Evian bottle into the coffee maker; *ting!* the lid comes off a cookie tin; *ziiippp* a pouch opens; *slip slap* water against the boat; *SSSSSS SSSSSS* the ceaseless rush of waterfall.

During our days together, my mind has been quick to

capture on the celluloid of my memory a series of striking images. As if snapping photographs, it has recorded precisely a sweeping view, a sudden expression, the colours of clothing, land, ocean. In quiet moments such as those when I first awaken, I review these images for my soul's pleasure, as if looking through so many favourite photographs.

I see Colin dressed like a buccaneer, wearing a bright bandanna and purple, swashbuckling nylon shorts. Looking relaxed and pleased with himself, he pulls a can of beer out of the cooler. I see myself shifting a rock in a shallow tide pool and watching dozens of tiny, thin-shelled crabs scuttle off in every direction. I picture the two of us stopping to catch our breath during a hike up a steep mountain trail. High above the ocean where the boat is moored at the dock, a trail cuts raggedly through an old-growth forest, which leads to an abandoned trapper's cabin and yet another waterfall. Heavy mud cakes our boots. The landscape is lush and deep, the setting fecund. Then there's an image of me laughing and hanging out the empty window of the old log cabin, looking younger and prettier than I have in years. *This lifestyle suits us!*

With the two-hour hike finally over, we stand—me behind him—in the spray of a waterfall that looms sixty feet over our heads, my arms draped easily across his chest. I remember a breathtaking view to the inlet below; I remember Colin pulling a picnic lunch out of his navy packsack. We sit on water-slick rocks and share our food. *"Water, water everywhere."*

Next, there's an image of Colin looking like the Jolly Green Giant, standing squarely on a massive moss-covered log, which has fallen over the trail, his arms raised in exhilaration.

Suddenly, there's a new series of images. A heap of items in the bottom of a dinghy, an empty champagne bottle, a woman's bright blue bathing suit, a man's Hawaiian swimming trunks. And there's another one of Colin—bringing my morning coffee and wearing nothing but a silly T-shirt with a fish saying *Bite Me*. Following this, there's an image of the unfortunate fish that *did bite*. Colin reaches over the side of the boat and scoops a nine-pound salmon out of the water with a net. Colin's eyes are sparkling blue, the fish scales dark opalescence. *Colour, colour everywhere.*

A long forgotten picture slips into my mind. Elements from the present scene resonate with those of forty years ago. *A man, a man with a fish, a man lifting a fish out of the water with his net* and the years implode. Reaching out to grasp the salmon that Colin has just pulled from the ocean, I feel the same slippery weight that I felt when I dropped a lake trout through the hatch hole of my father's wicker fishing basket. *Swoosh! In it goes.*

Similarities between the two men do not end here. I watch Colin as I watched my father 'get the job done' rather than talk about it. And like my father, I see Colin veer away from words as if avoiding a dead-head log in the water. Still, the scene is familiar and comfortable. Four days aboard Santana and except for a dozen other boats in Princess Louisa, this is our personal paradise. *After six years, I'm finally experiencing a west coast summer!*

On our return trip, we stop briefly at Thormanby Island where we drop anchor in the shallow water of the bay and swim ashore. As the tide rolls in, we wander along the remaining band of beach that connects the north and south portions of the island, knowing that it will soon be covered by water. The moment is mythical; we are passing through the mists of Avalon and the distinction between one world and the next is blurred. Within half an hour we will look back towards the land and wonder, *Where has it disappeared? Does the other world that we have been inhabiting really exist?* By the time we swim back to the boat, the beach is only an illusion.

Before pulling up anchor to leave the bay, before going our separate ways, we make love one last time. The compass needle points towards home but I do not need an instrument to tell me that I am feeling a powerful attraction to this man.

August 30 to August 31, 1997 **Gibsons, British Columbia**

re•new \ri-'nü *vb* to restore to freshness, vigour, or perfection; to make new spiritually; to begin again.

I awaken knowing that this is an important day. Eleven years ago today I was a bride, finalizing the details of my wedding before dressing in a Grecian-style gown. This morning I linger in bed, appreciating a sense of luxury before the day becomes busy and boisterous. With Nala curled up on my quilt, I admire the bouquet of long-stemmed red roses that arrived yesterday bearing a tiny card with four words, *Great Summer. Love Colin*

A song by Elton John comes to mind. "*There was a time I was everything and nothing all in one. But when you found me, I was feeling like a cloud across the sun. I need to tell you, how you light up every second of the day.*" Like my cat, I'm content in the knowledge that I am loved.

Reluctant to leave the comfort of my bed, I review the details for another celebration—tonight's—which is an *End of Summer Splash.* It is also the anniversary of Joann and me buying *Two Sisters*, our waterfront property and the venue for tonight's party. For the few people privy to inside information, it is also an early fiftieth birthday celebration for me, which has allowed me the pleasure of planning my own event and at the same time, warding off the possibility of an unwanted surprise party on the actual date in January.

The large third-floor suite is the perfect setting for the elegant dance party I've envisioned. *A room with a view.* Fortunately, it has just become vacant; we can think about renting it next month. But for the moment, everything is in order. Cake, band, catering and flowers. A friend who is visiting from Calgary will drive to Dahlias Galore this afternoon to pick up dozens of flowers, which we will place in glass sealer jars throughout the suite.

The dress I've chosen for tonight, a long bias-cut gown, will take me across the threshold marking the end of certain things and the beginning of others. *The end of my marriage to Brian and the beginning of my relationship with Colin. The end of feeling invisible and the return of form. The end of waiting, and in its place, creating what I desire. The end of isolation and instead, welcoming friends back into my life. The end of a tight restrictive world and the beginning of expansion and expression. The end of the first fifty years of my life and the beginning of the next fabulous segment.*

I leave my home and drive to the property, giving myself time to enjoy each aspect of the evening. When I arrive at the suite, I unlock the door, open the windows, greet the band, show them where to set up and talk to the caterers. Finally, I light the votive candles inside the Chinese-style lanterns, which I've made from brown paper bags partially filled with sand from the beach.

Party-goers presenting themselves at the front door are invariably drawn to the outside balcony by the shimmery shaft of light created by the lanterns that run along the wooden railing. The balcony quickly becomes the centrepiece of the party, offering guests an expansive view of the ocean.

The band begins playing; people drift from the balcony back to the living room dance floor. Someone announces that Colin and his friends, who have boated over from Vancouver, have just arrived. They've been attending the Indy car races this weekend and will return by boat again early tomorrow morning—to watch the final events—possibly even leaving before I'm awake. Their arrival adds a note of glamour and worldliness to the party.

I walk slowly down the long hall towards my lover; feel his warmth before he reaches out to hold me. *"And I can't explain, but there's something about the way you look tonight. Oh, takes my breath away, the way you look tonight."*

We link arms, return to the party and join the couples who are dancing in the crowded room. As I had hoped, the evening is light-hearted and sparkling. Around 10:00, while the band takes a break, we serve dinner and cut the cake, which is a version of The Little Mermaid cakes from the local bakery. The words, *Two Sisters,* are piped in squiggly script and matching figures frolic in watery-blue icing. Throughout the evening, Colin is attentive to the other guests yet never far from my side. *"It's that feeling I get about you deep inside. Oh, takes my breath away."*

Shortly before the dancing resumes, four latecomers knock at the door. Within minutes, the news they bring burns through the rooms of the suite like untended wildfire.

"Princess Diana has been seriously injured in a car accident. She might die!"

The mood intensifies, accelerates. The carefree feeling is charged with the sobering knowledge that life can change in an instant. Conflicting ideas and images clash for attention: the twisted wreck of a car, the twisted—possibly dead—bodies of the passengers, the magical setting of the party, the beautifully dressed dancers, the sensuous atmosphere. A heightened appreciation for living and loving is driven home. In my thoughts a curious connection is implied between our celebration here and those glittering parties elsewhere around the world attended by kings, princesses and playboys.

Finally, the evening slows down and comes to a natural stop. Colin takes my hand and leads me outside onto the balcony for a last dance. *"And in the moonlight you just shine like a beacon on the bay. And I can't describe, but it's something about the way you look tonight."* He leans towards me, kisses me gently. *"Takes my breath away, the way you look tonight."*

By the next morning, Colin has slipped quietly from my bed and returned to his boat. Princess Diana is dead.

Two women—both of them brides—have crossed over to the other side.

September 6, 1997 **Gibsons, British Columbia**

**floun•der \ˈflau̇-dər ** *vb* to act clumsily or ineffectually; to plunge into mud or wading; to struggle to obtain footing.

This past week has been surreal. Diana dies. My computer crashes, making literal meaning of my *End of Summer Splash* and in particular, the end of my marriage to Brian. A fax, which I dash off and send to Colin one night (intended as a sexy little note and one that will elicit a speedy response), flops and opens a Pandora's box to the past.

A few minutes after I send the fax, the phone rings. I expect that it's Colin, but it's not. Instead, it's a former lover I haven't spoken to in over a year. His call comes from out of the blue in every sense of the word—as he's flying over Iceland on a trans Atlantic flight. Perhaps it's the curious sense of feeling detached from the world that gives him the freedom to reminisce about our times together, for that essentially is the gist of his call. His grasp of long forgotten details surprises me.

"I remember us going to dinner at a restaurant on the top of the World Trade Centre in San Francisco. You were wearing a purple seamless dress. When you walked off the elevator, the mouth on every man in the room dropped open. You were so beautiful." I was twenty-five years old at the time. His warm remarks come after a long dry spell without many compliments and I'm flattered that he remembers me in such glowing terms.

When I finally hang up the phone, it's already past midnight. I decide that it's too late to call Colin although I know that he will have been trying to reach me.

Early the next morning he's on the phone. "So what happened last night?"

"What do you mean?" I ask, not immediately understanding his drift.

"I tried to call. I thought you'd like to hear from me after sending me that sexy fax. I couldn't get through."

"I was on the phone."

"I know you were on the phone. That's why I couldn't get through. So who were you talking to?"

"My stockbroker from Calgary."

He echoes my words as a question, "Your stockbroker from Calgary?" He pauses and then continues dismissively, "Give me a break."

"Yes, that's right," I reply simply.

"Well, then, what was your stockbroker from Calgary doing, calling you at 11:00 in the evening? What did he have to say for an hour that was so interesting?"

Things start to feel sticky. Mucky.

I take a stab at an explanation. "I had put in a call to him earlier in the week, to talk about possibly closing an account. It's been doing nothing but losing money." Then feeling the need to embellish, I add, "I'm really wanting to clean up everything in my life," before adding a final note, "you know, back to school, starting over and all that sort of thing."

"You still haven't told me. Who the hell is this guy?"

My old brain kicks in. *Danger! Protect Yourself! He's already suspicious after that party!*

"His name is Anthony. He was on an airplane, flying to Baghdad. He obviously knew I'd called and was getting back to me. I suppose he thought that it was as good a time as any. Besides, when he's on the ground, he rarely takes time for any sort of a conversation."

"What were you talking about?" Colin persists. Like a dog with a bone, he won't let it go.

"Actually, it was more *him* talking than me. He seemed to want to talk about old times."

"Your stockbroker wanted to talk about old times?" He echoes my words again and repeats his question, "So who is he?"

Red Light Alert! I struggle to keep my bearings and not get sucked into a swamp.

Sounds like a multiple choice question. Quick. Pick an answer. He's …

1. a stockbroker from Calgary

2. a friend

3. a former lover

4. all of the above.

I hesitate before answering, knowing that this is a trick question, knowing that either way, I lose. Either I become a woman with too colourful a past or a liar. I choose number four. "He's a man I had a relationship with twenty years ago and he's a stockbroker. In Calgary."

"And he wanted to talk about a twenty-year-old relationship?" Colin is incredulous.

Oops. Wrong answer. How do I get out of this corner and retain his goodwill towards me?

I try again. "Well, maybe when you're thirty-seven

thousand feet up in the air you have a broader perspective on things. Besides, he'd had a few drinks and seemed to be enjoying sweeping over the past."

"So, what does he want from you now?" A phantom lover hovers between us.

I reply truthfully, "I don't think he wants anything from me."

Still, I ask myself, *Do I want to be with Anthony? No. Am I still in love with Anthony? No. Am I pleased to know that he loved me? Yes. But that's the only meaning.*

"But you know," I begin slowly, wanting to speak the truth and at the same time, remain in the orbit of Colin's blessings, "it was important to hear him talk about how much he once cared for me. For me, it actually seemed to complete some old unfinished business. Things that had never been said before. It helped me put the past to rest. So in that way, I appreciate his call."

"Well, it sounds pretty weird to me," is Colin's comeback. "And I don't know why you didn't tell me the whole truth right away."

Why I didn't tell you the whole truth right away?

Because my immediate reaction was fear. Because I jammed up and couldn't think straight. Because I knew that either way I'd be judged. Because I thought it could ruin our relationship. How are those for reasons?

Instead I say in my own defense, "Listen, I've done nothing wrong and besides, surely you can't blame me for his call. Or for him wanting to fly off into the past."

The spectre of an old issue raises its ugly head. I recall shades of a similar scene with my father, when I was a six-year-old girl, trying to convince him that I didn't bite a hole in the padded dashboard of his brand new car. Finally, I realized that it was futile trying to convince him that I was telling the truth. It was not until after his death that I learned my younger cousin was to blame. But whether or not I was guilty, the damage was done. The suspicions stuck. The only thing I could do was try to earn back my father's trust in me, all the while waiting for his absolution. This incident with Colin brings up similar feelings of hopelessness.

I'm also bogged down over a decision about whether or not to renew my real estate license, which expires in a month. The policy of the real estate board states that any person holding a license must not earn income from another source. Therefore, any real effort on my part to begin building a counselling career is stymied from the word "go." Still, I've been anguishing about cutting off my connection to real estate which, for close to twenty years, has been one of the few constant threads running through my life. Not only has it provided me with a solid place to stand and a way to generate income, but it has also given me an identity as a competent professional, something which holds strong appeal at this time. Particularly, when there is little evidence elsewhere that this is true. I struggle against the heaviness of the week, hoping for clarity, but instead feel weighted down by soggy emotion.

Finally, it's Saturday, a week after my party and Diana's death. Sarah and I are at Colin's condominium. Today is Diana's funeral, which is being broadcast simultaneously on every channel I flip to on Colin's kitchen television set. I catch poignant images. A wreath of white roses and a card saying, *Mummy.* An honour guard of men—a duke, a prince and two young heirs to the throne. A man at a piano. I catch fragments of a song, *"Goodbye England's Rose, may you ever grow in our hearts."* Unlike the song, the unexplained pieces of the story hang in the air like discordant notes.

By early evening, Sarah and Colin have gone outside to build a beach fire. I watch them through the kitchen window and feel the irony of knowing that while my daughter is roasting wieners and marshmallows, another woman's daughter is being buried. *"Loveliness we've lost."* At the same time, my heart opens towards this man, and the young girl who sits beside him on a log until well after dark.

"And even though we try, the truth brings us to tears. All our words cannot express the joy you brought us through the years."

For Colin, being with Sarah is safe territory. With me, he's not quite so sure.

Vehicle

In my dream I'm driving an old beige van across a bridge. Instead of finding the usual equipment inside the vehicle such as a steering wheel, instrument panel, levers, lights, switches or brakes, there is nothing. The interior is a sealed fiberglass unit. Without anything to help me drive or show me what's going on, I become concerned about my safety. I want to get across the bridge and out of the vehicle as soon as possible. Furthermore, because the van sits high off the road, it feels unstable. The vehicle is cumbersome and nondescript; it neither suits nor satisfies me. It is simply a means of short term mobility. It will get me from here to there.

October 14, 1997 **Gibsons, British Columbia**

**strad•dle \'stra-dəl ** *vb* to stand or sit across something with legs wide apart; indecision; to vacillate between two positions.

Over the past five weeks I've travelled a rocky road. The recent dream image of a beige van and the idea of trying to drive without seeing what's going on inside, have left me feeling unsettled and alarmed. Fall stares at me like a blank slate; there is little concrete business to look forward to.

Early September promises new beginnings yet the memory of starting a new school year—with the dusty smell of fresh-sharpened pencils, the statisfying weight of packages of paper, and the exotic colours of Laurentian crayons—which thrilled me as a young girl—evokes only loss and feelings of being left behind

What's the use? What am I doing with my life, wasting it like this?

I drag my feet on buying a new hard drive for my computer (hoping that I can magically breathe life back into the old one), but finally accept that it is beyond repair. *Dead and gone.* Without a back-up disk, literally every word that I've written since I inherited it from Brian at the beginning of our marriage has been wiped out. Suddenly, there's nothing to connect me to the past. There's also nothing to stand on as an alternative.

I've struggled with another disappointment. The parenting course, which I was scheduled to teach through the community college, has been cancelled due to lack of sufficient registration. I scramble to get moving again.

On the spur of the moment during the first parent-teacher meeting of the school year, I offer to teach the same course in my home. To my delight, within ten minutes I have enough parents to fill my living room on a weekly basis. By the end of the first session, we have the makings of an excellent course: a relaxed atmosphere, enthusiastic participants, stimulating material and, for the often-harried parents, cookies and tea served in Old Country Rose bone china.

Although the current picture of the fall looks entirely different from how I imagined, on the other hand and based on the level of interest and energy that we generate in our weekly sessions, I know that this is teaching and learning at its best. Still, the antagonistic characters within me clash in a battle of wills surrounding my career choice and an end-of-October deadline that looms over me. Athena, anxious for the recognition that we would have gained by presenting in the community college, is not impressed with this more humble venue.

She complains bitterly. *"You'd be much further ahead sticking with real estate where you're already established, where some might even say, you're admired. And in terms of money, what you make in counselling is downright embarrassing."*

The Winter Gardener holds her ground. *"I think you're forgetting why we chose counselling in the first place. Don't you remember that dream?"*

Her question sends me rummaging through a stack of

journals. I find the dream I'm looking for in a binder labelled *Dreams: 1992 - 1993.* Rereading the dream five years later, I encounter the same teacher who challenged me back then for having the audacity to offer insight into a psychological issue she'd been discussing.

'If you think you're so smart,' she commented sarcastically, *'maybe you should take a master's degree.'*

Feeling humiliated, yet wanting to explain myself, I had offered apologetically, *'It's just that I love this stuff.'*

"There's your answer," the Winter Gardener states simply.

"What's love got to do with it?" snaps the golden goddess. "Besides, what have you accomplished in almost a year of writing in that silly journal?"

"We've endured and sometimes we've found meaning," replies the other woman.

Athena nails down the last word. *"Well, it seems pretty pathetic to me."*

While friends and associates have embarked upon a new fall season with a clear focus on where they're going, my gears are jammed and I'm looking through a dirty windshield. *Life is chaotic. Uncertain. Precarious.*

To quell my feelings of careening out of control, I begin my mornings by writing lists. Some of the items are ridiculously inconsequential but they are important, nonetheless, because each one contributes to a sense of substance, which I desperately need. The lists allow me the satisfaction of crossing off items and, at the same time, reflect in some small measure, my effectiveness in the world. Instead of driving aimlessly around town, wondering what to do next, I move tasks around on paper, hoping that one day I'II feel grounded enough to go into a store and buy Sarah a new pair of soccer cleats. *How can she start playing in the league if she doesn't have cleats?*

While procrastinating on some fronts, I'm a dervish of energy on others, particularly around cleaning and clearing. I rifle through closets and drawers, ruthlessly culling clothes from a former lifetime, which I suddenly can't stomach any longer, driven by the need to get rid of old clutter in the same way that I'd like to take a hard steel brush and scrub the skin off my body. *Anything to get rid of this feeling of constriction that is driving me crazy.*

Finally, I begin to see some bright spots on an otherwise discouraging landscape. Once again, I resort to a list to convince myself that what I've accomplished over the past few weeks is *substantial* and *real.*

1) Brian and I have finalized and signed our Separation Agreement. There is no mention of a trust for Sarah.
2) I've written for a year and kept a promise to myself to continue *winter gardening*.
3) I've rented the top suite of the waterfront building.
4) I've worked out an idea for a new embroidery that will represent *Rebirth,* the fifth and final stage of *Initiation.* In other words, I know where I'm going with this particular form of inner work.
5) I am well underway in creating my Christmas gift for Colin, the collection of poems called *Summer of Many Pleasures.*
6) I am finally in relationship with a man whom I love.

When I write down this last item in unambiguous terms, the realization of what this means finally hits home. Suddenly, I can stop and marvel at the richness that I've created in my life between Halloween of *last year,* when

I began writing about my struggle for meaning, and *this summer*, when I began my relationship with Colin.

Wonderful things await me and I am free to savour the satisfaction of everything in my life. This includes a romantic weekend at Hastings House on Saltspring Island that Colin has planned for me as an early birthday gift on the first weekend of October.

As I pack for our getaway (and anticipating the intimacies that we will share), I reach into my bureau drawer and select several pairs of new, black lace bikini panties. In a similar motion, my mind reaches into the past and remembers a dozen pairs of white, full-cut underwear that I purchased six years ago before moving to the coast. The contrast between the delicate items I now hold in my hands and the plain white pairs reminds me of a time when I had shut down emotionally and sexually.

Not long after I turned forty, I stopped wearing bathing suits and shorts in public. Not because anyone, least of all my husband, had told me that I should, but because these choices were consistent with the theme of covering up my legs, which no longer looked as good as they once did. When I brought the black lace lingerie home recently, I found the last few pairs of the white underwear stashed away in a bottom drawer. Still virginal in their original bag, I bundled them up and sent them to my seventy-five-year-old aunt.

Instead of boating to Saltspring Island like we did this summer, this time we arrive on a twin otter float plane. Within minutes of landing at the dock in Ganges Harbour, we've unloaded our bags, been greeted by the driver of a courtesy vehicle, and whisked away to the country inn overlooking the town and the same harbour we've just flown into.

We check in and are assigned our accommodation—a shake-roof cottage bordered by beds of roses, dahlias and cosmos. Colin unlocks the door and we step into the rustic warmth of a small elegant home. A bottle of champagne chilling in a bucket welcomes us. In the bedroom upstairs I find a bouquet of roses and a card saying, *Happy Birthday, Love Colin.*

For three days and nights, surrounded by the russet-gold tones of fall, we follow our own impulses. Wander along the slippery trails surrounding the property, visit the gardener tending his organic herbs, rent bikes and push ourselves over a twenty-mile course of rolling island highway. Other times we move indoors to light an afternoon fire, run a bath, change for dinner in the five-star restaurant in the main house, or pass on dinner altogether and remain inside to make love.

The physical intensity of this time together grounds me and the endless obsessing that has gripped my mind finally begins to abate. I delight in these exquisite days with Colin as I connect with my sensuous self. Something shifts in the core of my soul. Ambition becomes less urgent.

"Let's talk about Christmas," Colin suggests suddenly during our last dinner at Hastings House. "Where do you think you'd like to go?"

"I honestly don't know," I reply.

"We could go skiing," he offers, "or maybe you'd like to go somewhere warm."

The instant I hear the words *somewhere warm*, shame hot-flashes through my body. I groan inwardly, feeling suddenly paralyzed at the idea of appearing in a bathing suit at the pool of a resort.

My first reaction is one of dismay. *How can I holiday*

in the sun when my body is no longer beautiful? My second reaction is an impulse to cover up my feelings. *Quick,* a part of me urges, *pretend there's nothing wrong.*

But my tears betray my pain.

"What's happening?" Colin asks, genuinely confused by this change of mood.

I face a choice: reveal my vulnerabilities or continue covering up painful personal issues.

I take a risk. "I hate the way my legs look in bathing suits and shorts," I explain quietly. "I think I'd feel awful, having a holiday in the sun."

"I think you're beautiful," he counters. "I'd be proud to take you anywhere."

My sudden disclosure leaves me feeling raw and shakey. I can't continue talking. All I can say is, "Thank you," and try to muster a smile through my tears.

"It's OK," I hear him say gently. "We've got some time before we have to decide. You can think about it for a while."

The week following our visit to Saltspring Island is Thanksgiving but I have already given thanks for the blessings in my life, especially for this man who is unconditional in his love for me.

The beige van, which I saw in my dream five weeks ago, is moving forward once again. The path that I follow, like the one which pointed me in the direction of my journey a year ago, while still unmarked, has become less threatening.

Free Flying

In my dream I am skiing effortlessly along an open, groomed slope. There are no trees obstructing the course and it is not particularly steep. I'm pleased with the nice turns I'm making. I look good! Suddenly, I'm skiing very fast and realize that I'm out of control. I see a huge boulder directly in front of me. I know that I'm headed for a terrible disaster that could kill me in an instant. But in the split second before I hit the boulder, I manage to flip myself up in the air and begin to fly. Somehow, I've regained my balance. Although I'm shaken by my experience, I'm also pleasantly surprised to realize that I've survived what looked like inevitable death.

YEAR TWO

November 7, 1997 to December 18, 1997 **Gibsons, British Columbia**

re•lease \ri-'lēs *vb* to give up in favour of another; to relieve from something that confines, burdens or restricts.

Things fall into place in quick succession after my most recent dream. It provides the psychic impact I need to boot myself over the impasse surrounding my career—into the wide open space of self-determination. As I understand the dream, it is not only safe to leave the groomed predictable path but also necessary, if I want to enjoy the unusual gifts that my soul offers. Emotional turbulence had forced me to remain on the ground but the dream changes the forecast. The dense covering of cloud opens up; visibility suddenly improves. I can see my way through to a clear decision *not* to renew my license. Instead, I will trust that the process itself will keep me from crash-landing and gamble that I have the personal resources to chart my own course.

Energy that has been blocked by fear and the questions, *What am I doing? Where am I going?* is finally freed and becomes the fuel by which I *rev up* and *take off*. What this decision means for my sales work at the condominium project is that it will begin to die a natural death. What it means for my counselling is that I no longer need to be covert about developing my career.

As the season turns to late fall, I reflect upon the year's harvest: ideas demanding to be developed, insights asking for action, impulses pointing to a new way. Preconceptions about *how* things should be and preconceptions about *who* I am, are likewise challenged and undergoing change. These are the symbolic fruits of my labours, like jars of preserves on an old wooden shelf.

My parenting course, which at the beginning looked plain and simple, has taught me several important things. Listening to parents, I have learned how much they appreciate attending a course while their children are in school, when they don't have to pay a babysitter. I have learned that people love to be invited to join a group. I have also seen parents visibly relieved when I remain flexible around fees. With one woman, I accepted three exquisite Christmas ornaments made out of goose eggs in lieu of payment. I have learned that I can be emotionally open and still remain professional.

As I experiment with this more intimate style and allow Athena's exacting edge to soften, I finally feel like I belong to my community. Contributing to others in a directly personal way, I have moved from the peripheries of my life to plant myself firmly in the centre of my own existence. Through it all, I have survived my share of Psyche's daunting tasks and have deepened my understanding of the *Initiation* process.

I recognize that the time limit for my writing, which I imposed twelve months ago, was strictly arbitrary. *The soul does not blossom in one season.* And while I might be tempted to dig into the soil to see what is growing, I resist the urge, commiting myself instead to the continued work of *winter gardening*.

I contact Denise in Calgary and start making plans to deliver my first workshop called *Lives in Transition: Making*

Meaning of Change. In a matter of minutes, the date is set and the workshop is a reality. February 28, 1998.

Once I make this second decision, I start to fly. Working with pencil and paper as my only tools, I now understand that the soul does not bow, much less dance, to the dictates of dollars and cents. Soul responds to its own rhythms, its own beauty, its own form of meaning and I would be wise to simply accept this fact. But despite knowing these things, I long to defy the speed barrier and blast through to the final stage, *Rebirth,* in record time.

With this newfound energy, I'm impatient to start—and finish—my new embroidery. But the process of embroidering, like the natural order of all things, sets its own pace, demanding that I deliver thousands of tiny stitches in painstaking detail before I come close to a finished product. As this is the largest and most complex work to date, by definition it will take longer than any of the others to complete. Once I am underway however, the work will exist *in* and *of* itself. *It will be completed when the time is right. When the time is ripe.* My challenge is to sustain the tension between my longing and my eagerness to fulfil the process.

I begin thinking about where I could volunteer my services and develop my counselling skills at the same time. I call the director of the Canadian Cancer Clinic who invites me for a weekend training, which I hope will uncover rich material for another course that I'm developing: *Living Legacies: Making Meaning of a Life.*

I book a hotel room adjacent to the Cancer Clinic and invite Colin to join me after the first session on Friday evening. He's been out of town for a week and I'm anxious to see him. When I return to the hotel, he's waiting in the room.

"What have you decided about Christmas holidays?" he asks shortly after I arrive.

"I've decided that I'd like to go somewhere warm." I smile when I hear myself speak with such resolve.

"Well, then," he replies easily, "let's go to Maui. I'll make some calls next week and get things lined up."

My training at the clinic and my date with Colin creates a curious juxtaposition between life and death. I choose life and our love-making that night affirms my choice. Before drifting off to sleep, I whisper to him, "I'm so excited to give you your gift."

During the night, I dream that I'm in a crowded room about to begin reading from my book, *Summer of Many Pleasures*. The warm response from the audience conveys their appreciation. Appearing in public and revealing myself as a lusty sensuous woman, I'm proud to be approaching fifty years of age. In this dream-setting, I am relaxed, generous and delighted to be sharing my creative work. *This is my authentic self.* The dream validates the path I've chosen and feeds the Winter Gardener's spirit.

The days leading up to Christmas pass quickly. Between helping Joann at her store, attending school concerts and piano recitals, baking shortbread cookies and fruit cakes, I find a few hours to make Sarah and Joann matching flannelette nightgowns, which I've planned as a surprise for Christmas morning.

Whether it's the exuberance of the season or my intuitive sense that things are beginning to come together in my life, either way I'm propelling myself forward with an ample supply of determination and passion. By December 27th, my flying will be more than metaphorical. I'II be flying to Maui.

December 23, 1997 **Vancouver, British Columbia**

pitch \'pich *vb* to plunge down and rise abruptly up; to fall precipitately or headlong.

4:05 in the afternoon, the day before Christmas Eve. Sarah and I stand side by side, facing the full length mirror in my bedroom, pausing for a moment to be certain that we pass our own scrutiny before leaving to catch the 4:30 ferry to Horseshoe Bay. Our plan is to meet Colin on the other side and drive with him to the base of Grouse Mountain. From there a waiting gondola cab will carry us up the mountain to the restaurant nestled on top and the Christmas party of Colin's best friend, a local contractor.

Our eyes shine and connect briefly in the reflection in front of us. Smiling into the mirror, we see a mother and a daughter who bear uncanny resemblance to their own mothers as they were at this same age. Sarah is wearing a new, dark green velvet dress that is as beautiful as the matching plaid taffeta dresses that our mother made for Joann and me years ago. I'm wearing a black velvet cocktail suit that I bought five years ago in Calgary, a classically elegant suit that my mother would have admired and worn herself. My treasured baroque pearl necklace, which Brian gave me as a gift when Sarah was born, completes my outfit. I finger the pearls thoughtfully, noticing how they've already warmed to the temperature of my skin. I'm also wearing the diamond ring that was my wedding ring, recently resized and now worn on my right hand. I'm wearing it again after leaving it for two years in a tiny beaded box on the top of my dresser. As I look at the ring, I remember a comment from Colin, "You always act weird when you're wearing that ring." Still, the symbols of my status as a wife are hard to relinquish.

"So what do you think?" I ask, seeking Sarah's opinion.

"I think we look great!" she replies enthusiastically.

"So do I," I concur. We've passed our own test. "And now I think we'd better get going."

We dash through the house turning off lights. I grab our bag with the clothes and toiletries we'll need tonight when we stay over at Colin's home in Lions Bay. Sarah punches the code into the security system; I close the door and we drive off. Within minutes, we're parked at the ferry terminal.

Today, we're travelling as foot passengers. With Sarah's hand in mine, we walk towards the loading ramp, sharing a delightful sense of anticipation that wraps around us as luxuriously as the full length dark mink that wraps around my body.

As the ferry pulls away from the dock, I pull away from my familiar life on this side of the ocean: the easy lifestyle, the natural beauty, the intimacy between Sarah and me, the caring friends and family. We are travelling into the hub of a major city, towards people whom we know only casually. I am temporarily leaving my single life and travelling towards my lover. Although the ferry ride is only forty minutes long, the distance between these two worlds is vast. This is my first Christmas with a new man and I am not on solid ground.

The ship docks with a dull thud; the gangplank comes

down. We walk off the boat, down the maze of walkways, and out of the terminal towards Colin, who stands waiting outside his car, which is idling at the curb.

He greets us warmly, "You girls look gorgeous tonight!" and bundles us quickly into his car.

"And you look great yourself!" I return his appreciative remark, my eyes immediately drawn to the beautiful clothes he's wearing: the cashmere coat, the fine wool suit, the burgundy leather shoes and belt, the white shirt and silk tie. Clothes so entirely different from how I see him dressed on my side: jeans, polo shirts, running shoes and shorts, windbreakers, hi-tech sports clothes and caps.

Neither of us is accustomed to seeing the other in these clothes that refer to different times, different places. I experience a fleeting sense of dislocation and comment wryly to myself, *Will the real Patricia please stand up?* On the other hand, I have a sufficient grasp of the present moment to enjoy the very real pleasures of the tiny world within his car as we speed down the highway: the unmistakable smell of new leather, the tight purring efficiency of the imported coupe, the responsiveness of the vehicle under Colin's capable hands (the hands of a man who drove Formula race cars in his 20's), the distinct feeling of pride that Sarah and I are also in his capable hands, the feeling of safety, the note of sexual excitement heating the car more than the equipment under the dash, the scent of a woman, the smell of a man.

We pull into the parking lot, hand the car keys to an attendant, walk over to the base of the gondola, and present ourselves to the operator who promptly loads us into the empty cab. The automatic doors slam shut, closing out all thoughts of *the other side.* The gondola swings off the loading platform and begins its steady ascent up the mountain. Colin, Sarah and I are happily ensconced in our private coach as it sweeps us up the mountain towards a winter wonderland.

The mood of the evening is relaxed and gracious; the setting—stunning. From the wraparound windows of the restaurant, we overlook an immense vista of sparkling lights. When dinner is finished, Colin pushes back his chair and walks over to a window where he stands quietly. Seeing him leave our group, I realize that this is the time to broach the subject of Christmas morning, which Brian and Sarah proposed to me only two days ago. While I am aware that I may be tampering with the magic of the evening by bringing up their idea, I also know that time is running out. I leave my seat and walk over to him, place my arm gently across his back, turn to him and say, "Colin, I need to talk to you about an idea for Christmas morning." I've got his attention. He waits for me to continue.

"We were wondering—Brian, Sarah and I—if you'd be willing to let us have a couple of hours together first thing Christmas morning to open our presents ... just the three of us, so that we could be together as a family?"

There's no reaction from Colin. I continue, "Do you think you could go out for awhile?... for a run, maybe?"

Finally, there's a delayed reaction. I don't know what hits me first, his words or his explosive energy.

"What the hell are you talking about? You're asking me to get out of your bed Christmas morning so that Brian can come over and play house with you? Is that what you're asking?"

In the seconds that follow my question and his incredulous response, I see the evening, the goodwill between us, the present, the future and the man himself, fray and unravel before my eyes.

In moments like these when I attempt to straddle the gap between Colin's world and mine—between Sarah and Brian and my relationship with Colin—and at the same time, function as mediator, I feel my feet slipping off the footholds of land that I try to maintain on both sides of the ocean.

Unlike the infant in the story, *The Caucasian Chalk Circle,* who is at risk of being torn in two by women fighting over the maternity of the child, in this case it is me who stands the risk of being torn in two as I try to meet the needs of mixed agendas, mixed loyalties. With my loyalty to Colin not completely jelled, from where he stands it appears that I'm determined to continue deferring to Brian and his demands, wiping out Colin in the process.

The trip down the mountain bears none of the lightness of the earlier ride up. The gondola lurches and sways at it descends. My stomach, likewise, lurches and sways, queasy with the sudden sickening drop.

December 24, 1997 **Gibsons, British Columbia**

rend \'rend *vb* to split or tear apart as a sign of anger, grief, despair; to lacerate mentally or emotionally; to divide into contesting factions.

The next morning is Christmas Eve in Lions Bay. I wake up feeling drained and discouraged. Colin is already out of bed. When I wander into the kitchen he makes it painfully clear that he wants to get this day over as quickly as possible. The car is packed. Sarah and I are told to get dressed, to get moving. We're catching the 9:30 ferry back to Gibsons. Colin has decided what he's going to do.

"I'll drive you girls home but I'm coming back here this afternoon. There's no point in me hanging around your house where I'm not wanted. But Sarah and I have something to do. That's the only reason I'm coming over."

Sarah looks alarmed. We realize that we've created an emotional minefield. Feeling the weight of resignation and loss, I wonder, *What do I do now?*

The return trip on the ferry is rough in ways that extend far beyond the choppy water. Three people adrift on an ocean, we are uncertain of where to call home, where to find comfort, where to settle our hearts. Our mood is discordant with the sounds of Christmas as each of us scrambles to find an emotional footing. Colin is stone-faced and remote. I am berating myself, asking, *How could you expect Colin not to go ballistic?* and Sarah is attempting to repair the damage.

"Please, Colin, will you stay over for Christmas?" she asks. "Mom and me really want you to stay. Please, will you stay?"

"I'd really like to, Sarah," he replies quietly, "but I think I'd rather go home."

Her question hangs unhappily over the course of the day, begging for a reconsidered answer. Sarah and I alternatively confer or wrestle privately with the questions, *Will he stay? How can we change his mind?*

She is quick to apologize, "We're really sorry we made you feel bad." Quick to assure him, "It'll be really nice." And quick to stitch together the configuration of a family, "Colin, we really want you with us Christmas morning. We can all be there together, you and my mom and me, and Mary and my dad." She is starting to sound plaintive yet risks asking once more, "Please, will you stay?"

Shortly after we arrive in Gibsons, the doorbell rings. Sarah and Colin dash downstairs. I hear them speak briefly to someone and then close the door. Moments later I hear *klunk, klunk, klunk* coming from the direction of the carport—*klunk, klunk, klunk*—the sound of wood being heaved against wood. *They spoke not a word but went straight to their work, and stacked up the woodpile; then turned with a jerk.*

While they work outside, I remain inside, alone in the kitchen, praying that a man and a young girl can sort out the shambles I've created. I'm grateful for the brief respite that allows some of the tension that has built to a boiling point over the past day, to dissipate like steam from a pot on the stove. I imagine that Colin and Sarah are also immensely relieved to be doing something productive: something helpful, not hurtful; something enhancing, not diminishing.

Two hours later, Sarah calls out from downstairs, "Come and see what we've done, Mom."

I throw on a jacket and go outside.

"Merry Christmas," they call, their faces beaming as they stand beside a cord of wood stacked neatly against the wall.

"What a fabulous surprise!" I exclaim, walking towards them and pulling them close to me. "Thank you for the wonderful gift! And thank you for a gift that we can all enjoy!" Tears fill my eyes.

Suddenly, Sarah lifts up her head from our three-way hug. She grins and announces, "Guess what, Mom?"

"What, darling?" I ask.

"Colin's going to stay for Christmas."

I sigh with gratitude. "Thank you, Colin," I say softly, looking directly at him.

"You're welcome," he replies. "I think it's time to end this craziness."

At last, we have an answer to our unspoken question, *Will there be a Christmas?*

We resolve a tangle of issues with a series of quick telephone calls, sorting out the logistics of *who,* goes *where*, with *whom?*

"Who's coming to mass?"

"Colin's coming."

"Daddy's coming, too!"

Even though he's never come to mass with us before!

"What about tomorrow morning?"

"Maybe you should call Mary."

"Mary wants to come, too. She says she doesn't like not being invited, any more than Colin."

"Is Mary coming to mass?"

"No. Just the four of us. But where will we sit?"

Then noticing the time, I remark, "But if we don't get

dinner on the table, we're going to miss mass entirely. Remember, we have to be at the church at least forty minutes before it starts—if we want to find a seat."

I reach into a drawer for a packet of matches and hand them to Sarah. "Would you like to light the candles, darling?"

She obliges happily.

"You could also dim the lights," I suggest, "and then we'll be ready."

We take our places around the holiday table, which is decorated with miniature ornaments from Sarah's Christmas scene. Eight tiny reindeer dash down the centre of the table. Santa follows closely behind in a sleigh laden with colourful gifts. Clustered around him are carollers, snowmen in black top hats, children on tiny sleighs, Mrs. Claus waving goodbye, and barking dogs. Red plaid napkins and place mats welcome us to our seats.

Dinner is Christmas chowder with salmon, shrimp and sole simmered in a tomato broth and garnished with the fresh parsley that's still growing in a sturdy clump in the back garden. We finish with almond biscotti, coffee for Colin and me, and Ginger Ale for Sarah. "*Not a creature was stirring, not even a mouse*," and soon, in a twinkling, we were out of the house.

There are still seats when we arrive at the church. Over the following two hours, I push aside all concerns about tomorrow—about the logistics of the day, about the cooking time for an organic turkey, about whether I should give Colin his gift tonight—and allow the joy of the season to soothe my soul instead. Sitting between Sarah and Colin, I delight in the beauty surrounding me ... the familiar nativity scene, the stately candles, the extravagant poinsettias, the sweet fragrance of lilies, the musky evergreen boughs.

I wonder what songs we'll sing tonight? A quick glance at the numbers on the choir board satisfies me that we will be singing *O Holy Night,* my mother and her mother's favourite Christmas hymn. The same song now captures top honours with Sarah and me. Her hand in mine, we sing together—connected by a thread of words running between four generations of women—between this world and the world beyond. In this moment Christmas is complete. I have nothing to dread.

The day draws to a close. Sarah is finally asleep with visions of Barbie Dolls and Beanie Babies dancing in her head. Speaking quietly, I turn to Colin, "Let's go to bed." Before joining him in the bedroom, I pause briefly to unplug the tree lights, take two crystal flutes from the china cabinet, and pull a bottle of chilled champagne from the fridge. My preparations complete, I return to the bedroom to find him already tucked under my downy quilt. The embroidered pillows, which I had placed carefully on the bed a few hours earlier, have been tossed onto the floor. He has settled down for a long winter's nap.

"Colin," I whisper, nudging him gently with my words, "I've got your present. I want you to open it."

Slowly, his head and chest emerge from the covers. He reaches groggily for the carefully-wrapped slim package. I pop the champagne cork and fill the flutes. I hand him one carefully and try not to spill my own as I climb into bed beside him and make myself comfortable.

"Come on," I urge, unable to contain my excitement any longer.

He begins unwrapping the package, lifts the hand-crafted book from its paper and considers it quietly. Carefully turning the thick textured pages bearing poems and pictures of our summer together, he remarks hesitantly, "I've never received anything like this before."

Alarm registers in my brain. I try to make sense of what he's just said. Is he asking, *"What does this mean about you and me?"* ... *"What am I supposed to do with this?"* ... *"How does this compare with gifts you've given other men?"* Or am I just imagining this?

"Why don't you read it to me?" he suggests wearily.

"I'd be happy to," I reply, but as I speak I realize that the energy between us is flat. Reading aloud one poem after the other, I try to infuse the moment with the same spirit with which the gift was created. But with little or no response from him, I feel myself slipping away. I am losing that essential link to what I have been so intent on expressing, namely the depths of my feelings for him and my gratitude for what he has brought into my life.

Finally, it dawns on me. The man is overwhelmed. Too much emotion. Too much champagne. Too many words. He escapes the excesses of the day by falling asleep before I finish reading.

It is now past midnight on Christmas morning. I cannot allow myself to feel the depths of my pain, knowing that the words of my gift, conceived in love and wonder, have fallen on deaf ears. Nor do I want to admit what I already know: that, once again, we stand on uneven ground, each groping blindly for the other and finding no one there.

Until this moment, I could not see the irony that this collection of poems, offered to Colin as my own gift of the Magi, is delivered in a currency that holds little meaning for him.

December 25, 1997 Gibsons, British Columbia

spar \'spär *vb* to draw out one's opponent or to create an opening; to gesture without landing a blow.

I awaken slowly without the usual sounds of the alarm, cars on the highway, and the voice of a child. Lying in the luxury of my quilted cocoon, I savour the stillness and warmth. For a few exquisite moments the world is quiet.

My body seeks Colin's and I slide across the big bed, wrapping myself spoon-style along the length of his body. Conveying comfort, drawing comfort.

There's a tentative knock on the door. "Mommy. Colin."

The door creaks open. Sarah pokes her head into the room, "Merry Christmas!"

"Merry Christmas, darling!" I answer warmly. "Hop into bed with us for a minute." I flip back the quilt for her to climb in next to me.

"Merry Christmas, Colin!" I call out next, knowing he's awake by now, but preferring to enter the day gradually.

"Merry Christmas, Colin!" Sarah echoes happily.

Cosiness aside, Sarah can't wait to see if Santa came last night.

"Let's go and see if Santa filled my stocking ... or if he ate the cookies and milk. Come on!"

"I'm coming!" I reply, leaving Colin curled in the covers a while longer.

Scanning the living room, Sarah squeals with glee, "Look, he's eaten all the food and filled our stockings, too!"

She begins sorting through the presents under the tree, organizing them into individual piles: hers, mine, Colin's, her dad's, Mary's, even a tiny pile for Nala whose stocking reads, *Cats Love Christmas Too.* As usual, she will take charge of gift opening by handing out presents in an orderly fashion to make sure that no one feels left out.

While she's occupied with her task, I make a pot of coffee, pour a cup for Colin, and leave it on the bathroom vanity for him to find when he finishes his shower. At the same time, I wonder, *Why don't I ever take the time to shower and dress properly before we start opening gifts?*

A voice of reason prevails, "*No one expects you to be dressed up this morning.*"

By the time Sarah is ready, Colin has appeared, wearing the white Watergate Hotel bathrobe that Brian bought on a business trip.

Nice touch, I remark wryly to myself, appreciating the sly allusion to *that* break-in and *this* break-in.

"I don't have anything else to wear," he explains apologetically. "It's not as if I was planning to stay last night."

"I know," I come back, "and it's not as if you don't have lots of clothes. But at least I can wash your jeans so they'll be clean for Christmas dinner. What do you think?"

"I'd like that," he replies. "Thanks."

I retrieve his jeans from the bedroom, throw them into the washing machine, and the shut the door behind me so that we won't have to listen to the noise. Shortly after settling down on the floor next to Colin and Sarah and the pile of presents, I jump up again, saying, "While we're waiting for Brian and Mary, I'm going to light a fire." I grab what I need from the nearby bin, set the grate with kindling and wood, and start a fire.

Act One

Mary and Brian arrive. Sarah rushes to the door to greet them, dressed in her new flannelette night gown, which I wrapped in tissue and left on her pillow last night. Once we're gathered together in the living room, we start opening gifts under Sarah's supervision.

I have an idea. "Why don't we pour some champagne to go with that fabulous smoked salmon that Colin brought over yesterday?" Answering my own question, I leave the others in front of the fire and disappear into the kitchen to prepare the food.

A few minutes later, I return with a tray of smoked salmon, bagels and cream cheese, and pass it around. Fanning the fire of goodwill between Brian and Colin, I remark, "This is Colin's own salmon that he caught on a fishing trip to the Queen Charlotte Islands this past summer."

The comment prompts Brian to lift his glass and respond with a toast, "Thanks for your generosity, Colin." Throughout the morning, I feel alternatively like a gracious hostess and a cat on a hot tin roof, linking the men together through conversation and, at the same time, keeping a distance between them.

Presents are finally opened. We establish a time for Mary and Brian to return later for dinner and Sarah sees them off downstairs. I head in another direction, towards my bedroom. I announce, "I need a nap." This is my signal to Colin and Sarah that means, "Do whatever you please, only count me out."

Act Two

I fall into a brief sound sleep and wake up again after 3:00. The afternoon is turning to dusk when I climb out of bed and into a steaming shower. With half the day behind me, I'm beginning to enjoy a sense of assurance that there *will* be peace on earth, especially in my part of the world. Joann and Frank arrive shortly after.

I have dressed for dinner in clothes that are comfortable yet elegant, comfortable for working in the kitchen—whisking gravy, watching over braised cabbage steaming on the stove, heaving a turkey from the oven—and elegant for those brief snatches of time when I return to the living room to sit by the fire and talk to Joann, Frank and Colin.

"So, Colin," Joann begins, leaning eagerly towards him. "What do you think of your gift from Patricia?"

"It's nice," he replies.

"Nice!" *I can't believe what I've heard.* "What do you mean 'nice?'" I interject, looking directly at him.

His responce is brief and bitter, "Well, how do you expect me to feel about the gift after Brian tried to throw me out of the house?"

"What," I ask, my voice rising in disbelief, "does *that* have have to do with my gift to you?"

"Well," he replies, "he didn't exactly make me welcome, did he?"

"I can't believe what you're saying," I come back.

"If you ask me, there's something fishy about the whole thing." He closes the subject.

Stunned and struggling to understand his logic, which seems convoluted, I excuse myself, "I've got to check on the turkey." I stand up and walk into the kitchen, pick up a large spoon lying on the counter and begin lifting the still-warm stuffing out of the cavity of the turkey. In a reverse figurative motion, I stuff my disappointment back into a cavity within myself and suture it shut, quickly covering any tell-tale sign that this is the site of an injury.

Act Three

Brian and Mary return in the late afternoon. Sarah ushers them into the foyer and up through the house, past shimmering lights, flickering candles, sparkling ornaments. The turkey is carved; vegetables are ladled into warmed dishes and carried to the table. We're ready for dinner.

As we follow the gentle dictates of the name cards that have been set out on the marble table, the question we are all asking, *Who sits where?* is resolved quickly and everyone is spared a potentially awkward moment. Brian takes a chair along one side next to Sarah. I sit at the end of the table closest to the kitchen and Colin takes the big chair at the other end, opposite me. I am delighted to see him take this place and smile warmly at him. Throughout dinner, however, I know that he is uncomfortable. I also know that he's conscious of the time and looking forward to catching the last ferry out of here tonight, ostensibly to pack for our trip to Maui.

The End

I don't try to talk Colin out of his decision to go home. Instead, I help him gather his few belongings and walk him to the front door. Words are not only redundant but also inadequate.

In the aftermath of last night's aching disappointment and today's unsettling conversation, I am stuck between conflicting impulses. On one hand, I want to leave him in peace. On the other hand, I want to brandish his gift—the book of poetry—in his face and declare, "This is who I am."

December 27, 1997 to January 10, 1998 **Maui, Hawaii**

frag•ment \'frag-mənt *vb* to shatter into pieces; to lose one's identity or one's sense of a cohesive self.

Colin and I reconnect two days after Christmas. We meet in Horseshoe Bay and drive to the Vancouver International Airport to catch our flight to Maui. Despite the promise of the two-week holiday, which is my gift from him, I feel weary from the emotional overload of the last few days and slightly apprehensive. Grateful to finally board the plane, I find my seat, close my eyes and doze off immediately.

We land in Maui, pick up our rented car and drive across the island towards the Napili coast and our destination, The Ritz Carlton Hotel. We turn the car off the main highway and into the driveway that winds through acres of manicured gardens and lawns, drive past hundreds of flowering shrubs and trees decorated with tiny gold lights, and make our way to the front entrance. Massive torches on either side of the carpeted canopy mark our arrival.

A swarm of uniformed attendants descends upon us. Groomed and solicitous, they stand ready to park our car, relieve us of our bags, usher us along a richly-carpeted walkway. We walk past floral borders opulent with colour and fragrance, through huge double doors, past herculean floral arrangements, and over to the registration desk. The display of wealth is palpable. I'm already overwhelmed.

We finish registering and wait for a valet to show us to our tenth floor room overlooking the Pacific Ocean. We sweep past indoor gardens, jewellery stores and gift galleries; past intimate groupings of plush furniture; down endless hallways that are painted the same celadon green as my wedding china. *The same celadon green as my Crisca suit, which I've left at home in my bedroom closet.*

"Why didn't you bring that suit?" a voice demands.

Suddenly, I'm finding fault with everything that I've packed or omitted to pack, in particular, my peach silk peignoir and long gold dress, both of which are simple yet elegant. Instead, I have filled my bag with unrelated items of casual cotton clothing more suited for small-town British Columbia than for a first-class hotel. Pre-paid for a week, the meter begins running at a rate of $500 US per day from the moment Colin signs the credit card slip.

My former Athena self, dazzling and invulnerable in her protective armour, would have stepped confidently into this exotic world—knowing how to dress, knowing she could hold her own among the beautiful guests, knowing she was worthy of this extravagance and attention.

"How could you have forgotten those beautiful clothes?" she asks imperiously. *"Why didn't you know that you'd need them at the Ritz Carlton Hotel? Is your opinion of yourself so low that you can't give yourself the pleasure of wearing beautiful clothes, even ones that you already own? What has happened to you?"*

The massive scale and luxury of the hotel mocks me. In the brief trip between the lobby and our room, I feel increasingly tawdry. Like the country mouse, I want to scurry back home to my non-exemplary existence.

Suddenly, I hear my father's voice. The derision in his words is unmistakably familiar. *"Who do you think you are, putting on the dog like this? You can't afford this! You don't even have a job. You're just a phony thinking you belong here. And on a man's ticket, at that. You should be ashamed of yourself."*

Throughout our week at the hotel and the first week of our holiday, the weather remains dreary—not unlike my mood—as I contend with Athena's relentless criticism.

"Cover up your legs," she demands.

My body, once the source of admiration and personal pride, betrays me and becomes my shame. On a daily basis, I find myself plotting how to travel the short distance from our room to the pool. I grab whatever piece of clothing I can find to camouflage my imperfections and my despair—a sarong knotted at my hips, a strappy sundress I can drop poolside with an insouciant air, and various gauze items. Waiting for the inclement weather to pass, I spend successive days lying under a monogrammed towel, praying to be delivered from my obsessive thoughts and praying for the sun to come out and tan my body.

"Then your legs would look marginally better," she snipes.

"Get a grip," I hear myself say, but logic alone will neither release me from this hell nor show me a way to reach out to Colin in my misery. Fighting my own private furies, I don't even have the energy to make love passionately. When we make love on New Year's eve, I call him Brian. Disgusted, Colin rolls over with a groan. By the time we pop the cork on the champagne bottle and raise our glasses, the bubbles are flat.

Returning to our room each day with its tiny balcony, I feel like a bird in a gilded cage, surrounded by richness and starving for comfort. I am a wilder creature now and must take my pleasures more sparingly. I long to step off the glittering stage, away from the needless complexities of a world where room-service for afternoon tea and a scone costs $50. Try as I might to appreciate this generous gift, I can't. The excesses give me heartburn.

After a week at the hotel, we move into a condominium a few miles down the beach where I can walk out on the grass with bare feet; where Colin can barbecue his delicious meals on the front lanai; where I can throw on my bathing suit, grab my snorkelling gear and wander directly into the bay in front of the property; and where I can make my own cup of tea.

The gradually-improving weather allows us to be more active than the week before. I feel myself back on solid ground in more ways than one, genuinely enlivened to discover the abundance and beauty at our doorstep. I marvel at the vibrant flowering shrubs; the pink, red and copper bougainvillaea creeping along the walls of the building; a pool that seems reserved for our own private use; a bay bordered by tropical grasses and coconut palms; an underwater world to explore; hundreds of exotic fish to discover. Each day I return from snorkelling and record my sightings on a card from Snorkel Bob's where we rented our gear, noting with satisfaction the growing list of names. Yellow trumpfish, parrotfish, spotted pufferfish, ornate wrasse, racoon butterfly fish, gilder triggerfish, little bitty yellow tang and baby frog fish.

With each trip into this fascinating world of coral, lava rock and waving seaweed, I become more comfortable. I notice my body relaxing, my breathing growing steadier. I'm content to move around by myself underwater, identifying many of the specimens, which I now recognize. For those I haven't seen before, I make a mental note of their characteristics, which I hope to match up with the pictures on my card back in the condominium.

One afternoon I catch sight of a large dark shape and recognize it as a sea turtle. For several minutes I swim alongside it. My motions matching those of the turtle, I am filled with awe to be co-existing, if only briefly, with this denizen of the deep in its natural environment. The incident leaves me profoundly moved and quietly assured.

I run back to the condo and share my story with Colin who knows first-hand what I'm talking about from his numerous diving trips to the Cocos and Galapagos Islands.

Suddenly curious about one thing, I ask, "What was that thick ring I noticed around the turtle's neck?"

"Probably a mutation caused by chemicals from pesticides and fertilizers leaching into the water," he replies.

I shudder, understanding the implication of his answer.

"Well," he continues, "I'm glad you had such a great time."

"So am I," I reply, before adding, "and I'm glad I'm back," emphasizing the last half of my statement.

"Pardon?" he asks. "Back from where?"

"That's just a figure of speech," I remark. "I haven't really *been* anywhere, but for the last week I've been in so much inner turmoil, I wasn't really here. *Emotionally* I wasn't really here. Does that make any sense?"

"Not really." His voice is lifeless. "So what does that say about me, if you had to leave?"

"It's not about you," I reply, echoing words I uttered five months ago. "And there was nothing you needed to do. I just wanted to tell you what I've been dealing with."

Recognizing this quagmire and fearing that I'm already

losing him, I take a second stab at explaining, "Sometimes, certain elements in a present situation trigger a feeling from the past. When that happens, we might imagine someone speaking to us. It feels very intense—like hearing someone criticize us, for example—but it is really only in our mind. Still, it can be enough to throw us into a panic; we can lose our bearings for awhile. When that happens, everything becomes exaggerated and bizarre. Blown out of proportion. We forget who we are."

"What do you mean?" he insists.

"Well," I reply, "we might imagine our father saying something that is very painful and instantly feel ourselves falling into a black hole that we can't get out of. It's like having an old tape in our head that begins to play. And even though we *know* otherwise, we react as if it's real. You've heard me use the word before. It's called *fragmenting*. It happens to all of us. Instead of feeling whole, we fly apart, into what feels like a hundred pieces."

"For a week?" he asks.

"For a week, for a month, or for as long as it takes to figure out what triggered our reaction and get back to normal."

Watching him react to my comments, I realize it's time to drop the subject.

Figuratively speaking, I'm returning and Colin is leaving. It's as if he has said, "I'm out of here. This is too weird."

The second week in Maui culminates with us checking out of the condominium, driving an hour across the island and returning our rental car, only to find the small airport virtually deserted when we arrive there minutes before midnight. We're twenty-four hours early for our return flight to Canada.

At this particular moment, I am in better shape emotionally than Colin and set out to renegotiate our car rental, book another night at the same condominium we've just vacated, and drive us back across the island. Our holiday nearly behind us, Colin has spent a small fortune and undoubtedly feels royally ripped off. In the face of his considerable gift to me, I struggle to preserve a sense of value for my own gift to him and end up feeling like an ingrate.

Despite the unexpected delay, however, our final night in Maui proves fortuitous. I have a significant dream that I record the following morning before leaving again for the airport.

Turtle Goddess

In my dream I am visiting an old-style newsroom where there is much activity but also considerable disorder. I decide to ask directly for what I want. Turning to a man, I announce, "I want a job." He is not particularly interested in me but is willing to help in a perfunctory way. He suggests that I talk to a certain woman whom he describes as making more than $500 a day. My visit here is confusing and disappointing. It is a waste of time.

I find myself outside on a beach. I move intuitively to a particular place in the sand. I bend down and use my two hands and the length of an extended arm as natural digging tools. In a few easy motions, I uncover a dead turtle buried in a foot of sand. Examining the turtle, I notice that the flesh is still firm and well preserved. I pick up the creature and suddenly find myself holding the shell, which has separated from the body in a perfectly clean break. I marvel that the shell has come away from the flesh so easily and that it is completely intact.

This is a priceless object that I am holding—a gift from the instinctual realm—that is intended for me alone. I accept the turtle shell as a soul offering, understanding immediately that it is mine to retain and use in the world at this time. I also understand that I am to leave the fleshy aspect where it is. I cover it over with sand to remove any trace of its existence, thereby returning it to its source to be re-assimilated into the buried invisible qualities of the underground. I hear the message of the Turtle Goddess; she speaks to me through this symbol. I know what it means and my spirit rejoices.

January 11, 1998 to February 28, 1998 **Vancouver, British Columbia**

sow \'sō\ *vb* to plant seeds for growth by scattering; to set something in motion; to begin an enterprise.

We arrive home to find our coastal world blanketed in snow. We slog our way through mucky Vancouver streets in Colin's 4x4 and drive directly to Lions Bay where I pick up my car before catching the next ferry back across to Gibsons. We execute a quick turnaround; Colin piles my bags into my trunk and starts my car. Waiting for the engine to heat up, we stand outside awkwardly, struggling to grasp—trying to put into words—what we've just experienced over the past two weeks. There is too much content to compress so soon into language; the brain boggles trying to sort out the issues. Instead, we use time as our excuse.

"You'd better get going if you want to catch the 3:30 ferry," Colin suggests. "I'll call you later in the week."

I move towards him for a brief hug, "Thank you for the beautiful gift," and then I'm gone.

Like a migrating bird on its homeward course, my attention is drawn instinctively towards the other side of the ocean. Towards Sarah who's waiting for me at her father's, towards my life with its familiar comforts.

I collect Sarah and we're soon on our way home. We turn off the highway and onto our road, which is impassable. The snow is always heavier in this part of the town, yet for some curious reason, we're always one of the last neighbourhoods to be ploughed. But we've been through this before and know what needs to be done. We park the car next to the Canada Post mailboxes, grab our bags, lock the car and trudge down the road and into our driveway, fighting against knee-deep snow as we push towards our front door.

Sarah is thrilled with this unusually heavy dump of snow. For her, it means that the school bus won't be running and for me, it means that I'll be holed up in my house until I can access my car. My days will be devoted to keeping the home fires burning.

Out of necessity and until the cold spell breaks, life becomes simple, revolving around *not* unpleasant winter activities: walking Sarah to school each morning (virtually pulling her through the snow), which has become as heavy as cement, and keeping my driveway cleared so that when our road is finally plowed we won't be still marooned inside our home. I split kindling and talk "weather" with my neighbours while we're all outside working. With each successive load of wood, which I haul upstairs from the carport, I feel increasing appreciation for Colin's and Sarah's thoughtful gift. I cook hearty soups and stews with dumplings. Lessons—piano, dance and choir—go on the back burner for a week.

Once we're inside for the night, we enjoy an easy rhythm of shut-in activities: reading, playing cards, and the occasional game of Chinese Checkers, which prompts me to talk about growing up and playing this same game with Joann during the long winter months in northern British

Columbia. I share stories about my grandmother's early days as a pioneer in the Bulkley Valley. Turning to Sarah one evening, I tease, "If this snow lasts much longer, I'Il end up getting cabin fever like those poor pioneers."

"Did they really have a fever?" she asks innocently.

"No," I laugh. "But it's what happens when you're stuck inside too long. You start to go a little crazy."

A sense of good-humoured harmony exists between us. Despite my rugged chores, I realize that I'm grateful for them as a way to decompress after the emotionally-laden Christmas season. Thoughts of Hawaii grow dimmer each day like a quickly fading suntan.

Yet the dream, *The Turtle Goddess,* that I have on the night before our departure, propels me into the new year and into a new phase of my life, grounding me sufficiently to stay my course. By showing me a concrete symbol that I can readily understand, the dream has provided the spiritual impetus I need over the next six weeks to hold onto my vision of offering workshops on *change* and *transition.*

The dream opened in an old newsroom where there was nothing but dead energy. This suggested that, for me, the collective path was clearly *old news*. Furthermore, asking someone to employ me was futile.

While still in the dream, I moved outside and found myself in a natural setting. I not only knew intuitively what to do, but also had the tools—my own personal resources—to begin digging. I found the turtle effortlessly. As soon as I unearthed it, I immediately understood the meaning of the rare gift.

It's as if the Turtle Goddess were waiting for me to find her. With this thought, I begin eagerly exploring the multi-layered meaning of the dream. The shell and the flesh of the turtle are two distinctly separate, yet related, aspects of the Self. The shell, like the workshop that I've planned, is the masculine form with which to bring my work into the world, as opposed to the fleshy body, which is the feminine aspect: buried, largely invisible and mysterious. The dream confirms my decision to offer workshops on change using *Initiation* as the symbolic model for understanding personal transformation.

As a symbol, the turtle speaks of the interrelatedness of masculine and feminine energies. Each brings value to the other; each makes whole the gift, which would otherwise remain unrealized. The work of the feminine, which requires direct experience with the inner life (feeling, intuition and fantasy), is evoked from the unseen realm and substantiated by the masculine qualities of determination, strength and focus. Functioning in perfect balance, they join together to illuminate the work of the feminine and introduce a gift of consciousness into the patriarchal world. When overturned, the shell transforms into a chalice or sacred vessel that contains the potential for personal and planetary healing.

Throughout January and February, it is the power of this dream and my own resolve that enables me to tend the soil and welcome into the light of day, the seed of an idea that I first felt on a June morning as an impulse to present life-transition workshops. Once again, I trust the Winter Gardener's counsel and know intuitively that new life is germinating in my being. I know the importance of refusing to throw in the trowel on this idea. I know the importance of refusing to listen to my ego, which tempts me to abandon my vision.

"What if no one registers for the workshop?" it whines. *"What if this is a ridiculous idea? A waste of time? What if you're kidding yourself that this is important work? What if you're digging yourself into a hole? What if, what if?"*

Protecting this fledgling seed, the Winter Gardener responds with her own fierce retort. "*What if I my soul never sings? What if I bury my passion and heave my tools to the back of the gardening shed? What if life isn't worth living after I abandon my dream? What if I never know the joy of stretching out on a limb? What if, what if?*

"No," continues the Winter Gardener forcefully, *"I'll go with the gamble and insist that there is value in this work, even though it is mainly unrecognized and unrewarded."*

Still, the intensity of this inner conflict tells me that I'm in an archetypal battle between the old and the new; between what *has been* and what *might be*; between the former ego self, which is dying, and the emerging Self, who is struggling to be born.

From my knowledge of the *Initiation* process and from my reflections as I prepare to deliver my first workshop in Calgary on February 28, I recognize that I've arrived at a critical point in time. These are the dangerous moments preceding birth. Caught between nagging self-doubt and quiet self-confidence, from this vantage point of liminality—this sacred in-between place—I am able to look back upon the ground I have covered as well as towards the promise of new life.

I have embodied my own work through personal experience and can now locate myself slightly past mid-point along this continuum of change. I have travelled through the emotional territory of isolation, rejection and disorientation, and have suffered an onslaught of ordeals. I have moved, ever so slowly, from the meaninglessness of *Death* towards *New Knowledge* and *Rebirth.*

Her vision sweeping over the larger landscape of change, the Winter Gardener inspires me to trust that growth is occurring in the garden of my soul.

March 1, 1998 **Gibsons, British Columbia**

reap \\'**rēp**\\ *vb* to cut with a sickle, scythe or reaping machine; to harvest; to enjoy the benifits of one's labours.

Throughout this same period of time, Colin and I manage the bumps in our relationship in much the same way we manage the bumps on a ski hill. Occasionally, we are thrown off course; sometimes we fall; sometimes we avoid a collision; still other times, we enjoy the exhilaration of good skiing. We spend most weekends together in Whistler either with, or without, Sarah. Weekends with Colin are the antithesis of my introspective weekdays at home.

Time spent with Colin keeps me grounded and ensures that I don't drown in the amorphous world of the feminine with its dreams, symbols and watery feelings. An important part of his gift to me is helping me remember my athletic sensuous self. I welcome these invigorating days and recognize that I need a balance of concrete objects and activities as much as I need cerebral satisfactions. Ski equipment, lift tickets, hot chocolate between runs, homemade lunches in the backpack, a soak in the hot tub, even the smell of sweaty socks and ski clothes, or the satisfying smell of sex, become soulful necessities.

Simultaneously, I draw upon his physical presence and those same qualities of logic, strategy and strength within myself as I work out the long-distance details of my up-coming workshop.

Enjoining myself with bumper-sticker philosophies, *Feel the fear and do it anyway,* or *This is the time for the rubber to meet the road*, I marshal my energies. In varying words, these slogans tell me, *Just Do It!* and I *Just Do It!* Confirm registrations, tend to housekeeping details, finalize travel plans. I'll be staying with my friend, Denise, and using a large comfortable den in her home for the workshop.

I arrive in Calgary a day early to unpack and settle in. I try to contain my excitement. As I begin the workshop the following morning, I feel deeply honoured to be presenting work that I am passionate about. Throughout the day, I remain relaxed yet alert, excited yet grounded. *This is as natural as breathing! I am here! I am alive! I am real!*

As I bring the day to a close, I invite each of the eight women present to share her thoughts. One woman, a counsellor herself, refers her comments directly to me. "You are an embroiderer in every sense. From the exquisite intricate works of art that you have used to depict the stages of *Initiation*, to the skillful way you weave our thoughts and comments into the tapestry of your work. Thank you for a powerful experience." As I hear her remarks and those of other women, my soul wells with joy.

Yes, I intone silently, *this is the sound of my soul singing.*

Finally, I say to the group, "Thank you for the privilege of presenting my work. This has been a wonderfully rich day for me. Thank you for your generosity of spirit and your willingness to work in a deeply intimate way."

Whether I've worked with eight or eighty women matters not. What satisfies me most is knowing that *I have heard the whispers of the Winter Gardener and acted upon her wishes.*

Withstanding the rigours of the process, I have also gleaned new knowledge about a concept that has intrigued me for years, namely the integration of masculine and feminine energies within each individual. I now understand this idea more fully, not as an intellectual construct, but from my own experience.

It becomes clear. The feminine needs the masculine container to deliver results in the world, no more nor less than the masculine requires the feminine content as a way to serve the inner life. Through their union, the feminine receives backbone, the masculine, heart and soul.

I climb into bed that night feeling deliciously content yet still too churned up to sleep. I am also freezing because I have not packed a nightgown. Moments later I hop out of bed and pull on the same clothes that I've worn all day (and those that I intend to wear on my return trip home). Now wearing a long fleece skirt, mock turtleneck top and short boxy jacket, I jump back into bed and fall quickly asleep.

As I fly westward over the Rockies the next morning, I begin to appreciate the importance of this trip to Calgary and recognize that it marks the beginning of *Rebirth,* the final stage in the *Initiation* process. Like the initiate who returns to her community, often with a new name to reflect a new identity and a renewed sense of purpose, my return to Calgary brings me full-circle on this traditional archetypal path. I have left my city home to wander in an unfamiliar land; I have relinquished my real estate career and taken on a new professional identity; I have relinquished my role as wife and now stand alone. Presenting myself, at last, to my friends and associates, I am effectively asking for their blessing as I offer my gift, which not only makes meaning of my own ordeals, but also honours other women's experience. Symbolically, I have entered *Rebirth.*

Athena scoffs at my musings but the Winter Gardener stands her ground. She knows that it is precisely this larger-than-life quality that allows us to imagine that we are living a more noble life than our smaller stories of personal pain would have us believe. Through myth and metaphor we touch the transpersonal, connect with the profound. We enter the realm of sacred story.

I struggle to find words that capture the essence of my inner journey, but most miss the point. Still, I need the concreteness of words to reveal the Mystery and make my subjective experiences real. Without their supportive structure to attach meaning to events, I run the risk of missing what may be a transformative life passage; run the risk of seeing the experience dissolve like so many forgotten feelings.

The plane lands in Vancouver. I hurry off, grab my bags from the carousel, and make my way out of the terminal. As I step into the drizzly day, my eyes catch sight of a single yellow primrose growing in a concrete planter. Harbinger of spring and new things to come, this is the first flower to bloom following a long dormant season and the Winter Gardener rejoices.

March 7, 1998 to April 16, 1998

San Miguel de Allende Mexico

em•brace \im-'brās *vb* to accept eagerly; to adopt or take in with the eye or mind; to fold another in the arms.

The doorbell rings and Sarah announces brightly, "He's here, Mom." She dashes across the living room floor, turns the latch on the window and opens it. She calls down to the man below who is Joann's friend and also our taxi driver for the next two days.

"We'll be right down, Paul. Me and my mom are all ready."

Turning to me, she directs, "Let's go, Mom."

"I'm all set, Babe," I reply, picking up our overnight bag and closing the glass patio doors behind us.

We pause by the side of the pool and look up to the rooftop garden where Joann is watering her plants.

Sarah calls out in a sing-song voice, "Aunt Joann, we're leaving now."

Joann's head appears over the edge of the roof. She grins and waves, "Have a great trip, girls, and enjoy the pyramids. I know you'll find them fascinating. And don't forget to give Colin a big hug when you see him."

"We won't."

Sarah waves back, "Bye, *Tia.*"

"Bye, Honey," Joann answers. "I'll be waiting for you tomorrow night. See you then." She disappears.

Sarah and I hustle along the brick walkway of the inner courtyard towards an ancient wooden door and imposing wall that encloses *Casa Joanna* in a world within a world. We step into the narrow cobblestone street. The exuberance of a San Miguel morning greets us: cars honking, drivers jostling for space, women sweeping the sidewalks in front of homes hidden behind orange, green, purple and magenta walls, flower vendors pushing rickety carts laden with calla lilies, roses, carnations, birds of paradise. A band plays nearby.

Paul climbs into the driver's seat; Sarah and I take the back. The car bumps down the street, past *Parque Juarez* and women washing clothes in earthen basins, past teenagers shooting basketball on their way to school, past joggers running circuits. White garzas, perched high in the trees, are oblivious to the bustle below.

I turn to Sarah and smile, "This is a nice change, isn't it?"

She knows what I mean. Riding in a car is a luxury.

"How far do you think we've walked since we came to San Miguel?" I ask.

"About a thousand miles," she replies earnestly.

I'm not about to quibble; my calloused feet speak for themselves.

"But it's been worth it, hasn't it?" I comment.

She replies, "I really love Mexico, *Mamacita*, especially the school and my teacher, Teresa. She was so nice. Next time I'd like to come and stay with *Tia* even longer."

"Well, we can think about it. But for now, let's enjoy putting our feet up. And in about four hours, we'll be meeting Colin in Mexico City."

"Did you bring the photos?" Sarah asks suddenly.

"You bet I did," I reply, pulling them out of my bag.

"Well, let's look at them," she says. She reaches for the

first pile and flicks them onto the seat, one on top of the other like she's dealing cards.

We've seen these photographs before. Today, Sarah is more interested in a quick recall than an in-depth review of our experiences. Sarah selects her favourites from the pile. First, there's the two of us riding in the back of Pedro's truck on our way to the Waldorf school where we've enrolled her for three weeks. The school, an abode brick building, sits on the scrub desert of a private ranch. In the background is a curious sight: prickly pear cacti decorated with plastic bags tossed by the wind onto the thorns. Next, we see our Spanish tutor, dressed formally in a spotless white shirt and tie for our weekly lesson by the pool.

Here's one taken after a bus ride to our housekeeper's family ranch where twenty-three people (including Sarah) and an assortment of animals, cram into one photograph. Here's one that features handmade dolls bought from a Mexican woman wearing clothes that are curiously similar to those of the dolls. Another is a *fiesta* in *Tia's* garden with coloured streamers and paper lanterns.

The final photo shows the cathedral where we purchase miniature cookies dusted with icing sugar from nuns who live in the adjacent convent. Each time we visit the cathedral, we complete our transaction by sliding our money through a tiny opening in the wall and waiting until seemingly disembodied hands pass our cookies back through. The entire exchange is completed without words; the women have committed to a lifelong vow of silence.

Now, it's my turn. My favourites juxtapose unusual elements that mix secular with sacred, partying with religious pageantry. I pick up a photo of the central plaza at Easter. Everywhere we look we see colour: balloons, clowns, promenading couples, dancing couples. Music spills into the streets. In the background, the *Parroquia*, the elaborate pink Gothic cathedral with its pointed spires, looms silently over the festivities.

The next photo is taken inside the cathedral on Holy Thursday as parishioners enact *The Passion of Christ.* Men dressed as Roman guards carry flaming torches down the aisle and arrest the man playing Jesus Christ in the Garden of Gethsemane after the Last Supper. Statues of saints dressed in yellowing vestments gaze solemnly down on the congregation from plaster perches.

On Good Friday, we participate more directly in a second sacred pageant. We walk *The Stations of the Cross* through the dusty streets of Atoltonilco, accompanying yet another man chosen to play Jesus Christ. A small throng of visitors and locals wave palm fronds and carry rosaries and holy cards covered with tinsel and lace.

The photos that follow are suddenly sombre. The noisy procession halts abruptly at an outcropping of rocks designated as Mount Calvary. Two men from the community play the condemned robbers; they join the Christ-figure and share his fate in a symbolic death by crucifixion. A hush falls over the crowd as three wooden crosses are raised against the sky.

Sarah's been looking over my shoulder. With a sudden pre-emptive strike, she snatches a photo from the pile. "This one's disgusting," she declares, flashing it momentarily in my face before tossing it down.

It's a photo of me, sun tanning naked beside the pool. I laugh and our light-hearted mood is restored.

During our time in Mexico we've focused mainly on the simple, not unpleasant, logistics of living in a foreign culture. I pride myself on keeping the existential discontent of the past eighteen months at bay. The nervous buzzing in my mind has all but ceased, replaced only by the buzzing of mosquitos in our rooms at night. By the time Joann and I track down mesh netting to hang above our beds, Sarah is covered with welts.

"Remember this?" she asks, handing me a photo of the three of us walking down an unfamiliar alley, looking for a local doctor to prescribe an ointment for her bites.

"At least they don't scratch anymore," she notes with wry satisfaction. Then directing her question to Paul, she leans towards the front seat and asks, "Are we almost there?"

He answers in a lazy drawl, "My guess is, we've got about an hour to go."

"Well, in that case," she replies, "I'm going to sleep."

Mentally, I reach to push the Pause button. The car is quiet until Sarah wakes when we reach the outskirts of the city.

"Are we there yet?" she repeats her earlier question.

"This is Mexico City," announces Paul. "We'll have you at your hotel in no time."

Fifteen minutes later, Sarah and I are waiting for Colin in the lobby of the Majestic Hotel, sitting on the edge of a stone fountain. She spots him coming through the door. In a flash, she's in his arms. A moment later, I'm there with her.

"And this one's for Aunt Jo," she says, giving him another squeeze.

He laughs, "So, who's ready to look around the city?"

"We are," Sarah pipes in.

"Well, then, let's leave our bags in the room and get going." He moves towards the elevator; we follow closely.

Opening the door to our room, he pauses and turns to me, remarking mysteriously, "By the way, I have a gift for you." Allowing the suspense to build, he slowly pulls a blue velvet box out of his bag and hands it to me.

A question flashes through my mind, *Is he giving me an engagement ring?* I panic for a second.

"Don't be so silly," a voice shoots back. *"Hurry up. Open the box."*

Sarah cheers me on, "Come on, Mom, just open it."

I raise the lid of the tiny box and peer cautiously inside, finding *not* a diamond ring, but a handcrafted silver ring moulded in the shape of a turtle.

I laugh and the tension evaporates. "It's beautiful, Colin," I say as I slip it on my index finger and reach up to kiss him. "And it's the Turtle Goddess. What a sweetheart you are, remembering what the turtle means to me. Thank you. Thank you." I plant another quick kiss on his lips.

The afternoon is an abbreviated walking tour of the city. We begin at the Zocalo Templo, exploring the ruins of an ancient city that electrical workers discovered under the plaza in 1970. Finally, we visit the National Palace and the towering murals of Diego Rivera, which chronicle the history of Mexico from the arrival of the Aztecs to the revolution. By the time we return to the hotel, we are weary and hungry and relieved to hear that we can order a simple dinner in the roof-top restaurant.

"I'm tired, Mommy," Sarah says before too long.

Colin picks up the bill, pays our server and we return to our room. Within five minutes, Sarah is in her pyjamas, she's brushed her teeth, kissed us and jumped into her cot at the foot of our bed. A moment later, her steady breathing tells us she's already asleep. That's our cue to get into bed ourselves.

I nestle against Colin's chest, basking in the pleasure of his closeness, not wanting to move.

"Te quiero," I whisper seductively.

Colin laughs quietly, his lips warm against my cheek, "Pardon me?"

My voice husky and low, I reply, "I love you, I want you."

"What do I say?" he asks.

"You could say, *Tu eres mi cielo* ... 'you are my heaven.'"

He takes a stab at it, *"Tu es mi cielo."*

"That's pretty close," I laugh.

"What else?" he asks.

The novelty of the setting—the hotel room, the sleeping child, the foreign city—creates an outrageous mood.

I turn up the heat, *"Por favor, yo quiero estar desnuda,"* pausing before adding the English equivalent, "'I want to be undressed.'"

"Tell me more," he encourages, nuzzling me closely.

My voice is barely audible. *"Poséeme ya."*

"And *that* means?" Colin asks suspiciously.

"'Take me. Hard.'"

He sputters, then remembering Sarah, stifles a loud guffaw. "Christ, woman, you are some lady!"

"Gracias, mi guapo," I reply demurely.

I've just about depleted my repertoire. I lay down a final ace card, *"Qué mango!"*

"Sounds juicy to me," he replies, waiting for an explanation.

"Well," I tease, "this is a rough translation, but it's something like 'what a handle.'"

You learned *that* from your Spanish tutor?" Colin asks incredulously.

Pressed to disclose, I comment simply, "One of Joann's friends has a new Mexican boyfriend."

I return linguistically to the beginning and invite him again, *"Te quiero."*

He knows enough Spanish to say, *"Si, Si,"* then adds jokingly, "my heaven."

The next morning Paul returns to drive us to Teotihuacan, the immense archeological site that was a thriving city in the sixth and seventh centuries. We spend the day in the blistering heat, visiting palaces and plazas, and walking along the Avenue of the Dead—the same route that inhabitants of the great city, as well as sacrifice victims—would have walked centuries ago during ceremonies and religious rituals. Long after we climb the monumental staircase of the Temple of the Moon and are driving back to San Miguel, the fine film of grit covering my skin reminds me of this remarkable period in Mexico's rich history.

It's past 11:00 when Paul drops us off at Joann's front gate. She greets us in the courtyard.

"Is anyone hungry?" she asks, walking towards the house with her arms around Sarah and Colin. "I've got some cold chicken and salsa and tortillas. How does that sound?"

Sarah is suddenly wide awake; she speaks for us all. "That sounds yummy."

"OK, let's get some food. Then we'll all sleep well. At least until the birds start chattering. Isn't that right, Sarah?" *Tia* says, winking at her.

Once our late-night snack is finished, Colin declares, "I've had it. I need some sleep."

"So do I," replies Sarah, leaving with Joann to go upstairs. Colin and I turn towards my bedroom and the massive rough-carved bed that commands most of the room.

"What was that Spanish expression?" he asks, pulling me close."

"Yo quiero estar desnuda."

He chuckles to himself.

I fall into a deep sleep, only to awaken in the middle of the night, hot and sticky inside the mosquito netting which drapes over the four bed posts. Colin is still asleep, his body flung across his side of the bed. My mind grabs onto a story from Mexico's turbulent past; my imagination embellishes it.

The year is 1810. Father Hidalgo de Costilla lies on a similar rough-carved bed, plotting Mexico's independence from the Spaniards just hours before he will stand in front of his congregation in Cocomacan to make an impassioned cry for freedom. His body splayed across the bed, naked and sweating, he struggles with the dark night of his soul.

I imagine him asking, "Is this what Spirit intended for my life? Must I drink from this cup or can I push it away?" And finally, "Dear God, do not forsake me." Hidalgo's words could be mine.

For now, however, I'm content to spend the last couple of weeks at *Casa Joanna* with Colin, topping-up our Mexican holiday. He leaves three days before we do. When our own plane finally taxis down the runway, preparing for take-off, I'm ready for take-off myself. Rested and refuelled with the potent power of solar energy, I'm anxious to press Fast Forward.

April 17, 1998 to April 20, 1998 **Vancouver, British Columbia**

gath•er \'ga-thər *vb* to collect; to recover or acquire strength; to come to a head, develop purulent swelling.

We're back on *terra firma,* tired but happy, standing in the baggage area of the Vancouver International Airport next to the sign, *JAL Arrivals From Mexico City,* waiting for the luggage chute to open and disgorge our belongings. With a luggage cart parked in front of each of us, we're poised and ready to collect the eleven assorted bags and boxes that Sarah tallied at the check-in counter.

Her new language skills still fresh, she wields a rudimentary Spanish. *"Uno, dos, tres,"* she speaks excitedly as the first three items appear. Joann grabs them and heaves them onto her cart. The rest of our belongings arrive in close succession. Everything is collected. We push our teetering carts towards the customs officer who gives our pink slips a perfunctory glance and waves us through. We're sent on our way.

"See if you can find us a cab," I say to Sarah as we swing out through the automatic doors leading into the waiting area of the terminal.

"Taxi, por favor," she quips proudly. We laugh as she

ditches her cart and scoots away to look for the taxi queue. A minute later, she returns with an even better idea.

"*Mamacita*, there's a big white limousine out there with a sign on the trunk saying *For Hire*. Can we take it? Oh, please, *Mamacita?*"

The limousine is the ideal way to move our monstrous pile of belongings to our cousin's home where Joann and I have left our cars. It's luxurious and at the same time, more affordable than hiring two cars. We jam our baggage into the vehicle. Finally, we settle into the plush seats, close the doors behind us, and breathe grateful sighs as the uniformed driver pulls away from the curb and away from the hubbub of the travellers' world. Feeling immensely satisfied, each of us has been filled to overflowing with the impressions of Mexico: colour, love, laughter, language and history. Two women and a young girl, we can call ourselves intrepid travellers.

Despite our feelings of worldliness, however, now that we are only an hour's drive plus a forty-minute ferry ride away from home, we can't get there fast enough. The minute that Sarah and I arrive home, the pace of life speeds up.

Pets and friends demand time and attention. Nala expresses her indignation over our extended absence by meowing loudly and rubbing against our legs. Cameron, the boy from across the street who has been taking care of our pets, wastes no time in knocking on the door to collect his wages and return the hamster that has been boarding at his house. I stand in the foyer, holding the hamster cage, with boxes and bags all around me. Life at home as we have known it, is already encroaching upon our Mexican experience.

I try to resist this intrusion of reality yet at the same time, when I gaze at my four white walls, I realize that I want more colour in my life. *Colour*—like I saw everywhere in Mexico—on walls, doors and buildings—*infuses my soul*. Immediately, I start thinking about painting certain rooms in my house.

Sarah heads outside to play kick-ball with children in the neighbourhood. This is a good time to call Colin in Lions Bay, to tell him that we've arrived home safely. I'm delighted to reach him directly.

"Hi," I say excitedly, "we're home. In one piece."

A silence opens up. I wait for his response.

"Why didn't you stop at my house on your way home instead of going straight to the ferry?" he asks. "You know it's only fifteen minutes from the ferry."

"Quite honestly, I never thought about it. We were just so anxious to get home. I wanted to start unpacking some of our gear."

"Well, you know I'm leaving for Costa Rica in two days and I'll be gone for almost a month. I'd have thought you'd want to see me."

All colour drains from the day. Energy drains from my body.

"I do want to see you," I insist weakly. "That's why I'm calling."

Suddenly, I'm floundering. *What am I doing wrong? Why am I always disappointing him? Injuring him? Is there some rule that I'm not aware of, that I'm breaking?*

"Well," I protest aloud, "why didn't you tell me when you left Mexico that you'd like us to stop over on our way home? You could have done that, you know."

"Don't you think you could have figured that out for yourself?" is his comeback.

"I guess I could have," I admit quietly. Attempting to

mollify him and at the same time, salvage the moment, I push on, "Well, do you think you could come over and see us tomorrow? Stay a night or two with us?"

A pause, "I suppose I could do that." The conversation ends on a faded note. By now, I want nothing more than a numbed sleep that will ease my feelings of panic.

During the night, a voice speaks out in a dream. *"I want my own electricity."*

Red Light Alert! Red Light Alert! Alarm registers in my dream-body. With a sharp sudden jolt, I'm wide awake. I repeat the words I've just heard, "I want my own electricity." My mind grapples to connect these words with ideas that I heard at a workshop in Mexico. A trainer was presenting the work of Dr. Caroline Myss, author of *Anatomy of the Spirit: The Seven Stages of Power and Healing.*

Electricity. Energy. The words link directly to my conversation with Colin last night and explain what was happening between us in that brief unsatisfactory exchange.

"Wake up," the dream seems to be saying, "you are losing essential energy." Delivered as a simple startling punch, it confirms my sense that energy was draining from my body. But equally alarming is the *meaning* of this loss of energy. From my counselling work, I realize that this loss of energy implies a loss of connection to Self, which is the greater source of my alarm. My response is visceral, like an animal smelling danger.

I fall back into an unsettled sleep and wake in the morning with a blinding migraine. The pounding in my brain is so excruciating, I think I'm having a cerebral hemorrhage. Waiting for Colin to arrive off the ferry, I push aside the boxes and bags crowding the foyer, carving a narrow path through the obstacles in much the same way I push aside any niggling thoughts about the dream message. Later in the day when Colin comments that I seem "spacey," I mutter something about still being on "Mexican time" and hope that it holds as an excuse.

Although it has been only five days since Sarah and I saw him off in Mexico, when we meet there is a sense of needing to bridge a gap between us. Making love that night, our bodies are eager to dispel any disquiet we may feel, eager to press a skin-to-skin imprint upon the other. Our intimacy renews a pact between us, reassures us. *Yes, we have a relationship. Yes, this is the man, this is the woman, I love. Yes, this is where I love.* The sensory memory will have to suffice for the next three weeks while Colin is away.

Monday morning after Colin leaves to catch the ferry home, I call the community school where (before leaving for Mexico), I have been scheduled to present two workshops: the nine-week training, *Developing Capable People*, and my new one-day workshop, *Lives in Transition:Making Meaning of Change.*

"Stacia, this is Patricia," I announce. "I'm just back from Mexico and wanted to check on registrations for my programs."

"Good news!" she responds enthusiastically. "We've got thirteen people signed up for the parenting course and seven women have registered for your *Lives* workshop."

I can't believe my ears. I hesitate for a second, struggling to process this unexpected news. "My God, that's fabulous!" I finally say. My mind reaches for logistics to steady itself. "Well, then, I guess I'll see you later in the week. The first session starts Thursday, doesn't it?"

"Yup, you've got it!" She nips the conversation, "See you

then," and she's gone.

Incredulous, I drop the phone down onto the receiver and exclaim, "I can hardly believe it!"

Instantly, the Winter Gardener grasps the meaning of what she's just heard. After almost two years of struggling to produce the poorest of specimans from the soil around her, after nourising herself with only the most meagre of sustenance, the Winter Gardener feels richly rewarded.

This is the manna, this is the sweetness, this is the joy that is the promise of Initiation. As the soulful fruits of her labours, this is a bouquet that surpasses anything she might have seen in the Maui Ritz Carlton Hotel.

Blessed with the early bounty of *Rebirth* and the guidance of the Winter Gardener, I finally stand upon a foundation that feels firm underfoot.

This is a foundation that will inform my life and support my growth.

May 15, 1998 to May 16, 1998 **Gibsons, British Columbia**

swamp \'swämp *vb* to inundate; to overwhelm by an excess of something; to submerge as if with water.

The past three weeks have flown by. My energy has been amplified by the pleasure of teaching my parenting course, by the glowing feedback I've received from people taking the course, by feeling connected to my community, and by feeling that my contributions are valued. I am also anticipating Colin's return when I will show off the results of my first foray into house painting. Taking my inspiration from my trip to Mexico, I've painted most of my house: the foyer, the main living area, my bedroom and Sarah's bedroom. Each room has been transformed into a warm oasis of colour.

I'm alive! I'm in love—with life, with my work, with creativity, with my lover who returns tonight!

I marvel at the richness of my life today and pinch myself to remind me that it's real. Looking back at the beginning of this strange journey that I have since identified as *Initiation,* remembering the bleak landscape that I inhabited over the fall of 1996 and into the winter of 1997, the contrast seems surreal. I recall my despair during the *Death* stage, when I could see no prospects on the horizon, neither personal nor professional; when I had no sense of direction and even less sense of identity. Terror, as my constant companion, inflamed my fears that I would never have the life I desired: fulfilling work, a lover and companion, and creative expression to put a patina on my life.

When the door bell rings, it's Colin who has just arrived from the ferry. I open the door, throw my arms around him and step into his embrace.

"Come on," I urge, grabbing him by the hand and hauling him upstairs, "I want to show you how I've painted my bedroom. In every one of these rooms," I continue, pointing out the areas that I've painted as I lead him through the house, "it took me at least two stabs at colour—two coats of paint, that is, sometimes three—before I finally got it right."

We're standing at my bedroom door. "What do you think?" I ask, insisting on a response.

"Well," he says slowly, "it looks better."

I'm confused. This doesn't compute. I repeat his words as a question and direct them back to him. "It looks better?" Then I snap an angry retort, "I can't believe that's all you can say."

I've lost my train of thought, swerve unexpectedly, "Well, would you like to stay here tonight? We could both leave early in the morning when I head off to present my workshop."

"No," he replies, "I'd rather spend the night at the condo. I'll meet you out there tomorrow after you're finished."

"Whatever you want," I reply curtly. *I don't want to get embroiled in this tonight, not before my workshop.*

He leaves shortly afterwards. I close the door behind him, hoping to blot out the residual discomfort from this conversation. Instead, my mind begins to twist on ideas.

If I could cut below his comment, would I hear him say,

"Why would a crummy bit of paint make me feel any differently about your house?" Would I hear him say, *"I hate your fucking house, hate everything about it."* Would I hear him say, *"I feel like your goddamned husband's still in the bedroom. Why would I want to stay in another man's house when I have two homes of my own?"* Or would I hear him say, *"Come with me and be my love?"*

But without the benefit of understanding what he's really saying, I'm left feeling half-sick and half-disgusted by his pallid remark, "It looks better."

I wish that I had railed at him, "Why, in hell, can't you just tell me what you mean?"

Despite the incident, the workshop the next day is excellent. As I listen to women's comments during the closing exercise, the ground upon which I stand is solid and satisfying. Words take shape around the feelings stirring in my soul. *This is right and good. This is my Work.* The Winter Gardener feels doubly blessed, knowing that she also nourishes those around her.

My materials collected and stowed in the car, I drive to Colin's condominium.

"How was your workshop?" he asks, greeting me at the door.

"It was fabulous," I come back. "And thank you for asking. I love presenting this work and even now, I'm not feeling tired. So, yes, it was wonderful."

"Good for you." He smiles and continues, "Well, these are my thoughts for the evening. After dinner, let's take a walk down the beach, watch the sun set, and then go to bed early. Make love."

A groan of pleasure escapes from my throat.

Darkness is descending as we return from the beach, kick

off our sandy shoes at the door, turn off lights, and climb the stairs to his bedroom.

"I'll run a bath for you," he offers easily. In a minute I hear the water running.

I step into his bedroom. The room is a dark sensuous jewel. Wide windows open to an immense night view; distant lights line a remote horizon. Two small oil lamps, globes of emerald green glass, one on either side of the bed, cast warm spheres of light. The room smells of fresh linen. My readiness for this moment tells me, *This is where I want to be.*

Colin calls out, "Your bath is ready." I move towards the bathroom where the air is warm and luxurious with the scent of musk. A pampered woman, I strip off my clothes and slide into the tub. "My God, this is wonderful," I mutter to myself, revelling in the idea of joining my lover shortly.

I stretch out—languid and lazy—in the steaming water and close my eyes. Time floats away. Suddenly, Colin is standing in the room. His words chafe against the texture of the moment.

"So what are you going to do if you run into Charles this summer?"

"Pardon me?" *I can't believe I'm hearing this.*

He repeats himself, "So what are you going to do if you run into Charles this summer? I know he and his wife always come to the coast for a month or two."

The mood of our reunion begins to dissolve like coloured bath crystals. Suddenly, I'm struggling to keep my head above water.

Anger flares inside me; we've hashed over this incident too many times. "I haven't a clue," I reply, "and it doesn't matter. I'm not some hapless woman who can be plucked off against my will. I'm not at risk of having my virtue compromised. Whatever the situation is, I can handle it."

"Well, that's not how I saw it last summer, the way you two were carrying on. That was pretty stupid."

"It wasn't stupid," I object, "but it certainly didn't produce the effect I wanted."

"Well, it *was* stupid." He emphasizes his point, then continues, "And what about the way you handled that telephone call with Anthony? Don't you think that was wrong—not telling the truth right away?"

"Right or wrong, it's got nothing to do with you and me now. And I told you at the time, I'm not interested in him. Not interested in either of them."

The bathroom, which only moments before was a pool of intimacy and promise, takes on a nightmarish quality.

I stand in a steamy jungle, lost and disoriented, hacking with a flashing machete at the twisted tangled growth that has sprung up around me. Towering above the bath, Colin reaches into an unwieldy black bag that he has dragged in—a bogeyman's bag—and lifts out each of the various injuries that I've perpetrated against him.

He asks, "Why did you do *this*? And *this*? And *this*? Why do you always ruin everything that's good?"

"Can't we just drop this whole thing?" I implore, fighting to keep myself from sinking into the quicksand of this conversation. At the same time, I struggle to understand him. "Please trust that I can handle my own affairs."

"I'm just asking you to do one thing," he says.

"And that is?" The question hangs in the air.

He replies, "Not to talk to Charles. Not to see him."

I pause. "That feels like a box. And my life already feels

constricted enough. Besides, in a small town, that's pretty hard to do."

"I don't ask you to do very much for me," he pushes on.

"No, you don't," I agree. My words slow down; my voice becomes quiet. "But you also don't need to tell me how to deal with Charles, for instance. To be quite honest, I'm pleased with the way I'm managing my life these days. And when something goes off the rails, I'm pretty quick to straighten it out.

"I guess what I'm talking about is *autonomy,"* I continue quietly. "*That's* what this is about. And with autonomy, you don't need to tell me what to do. I can be my own judge of that."

He lashes out, "Oh, you mean you do whatever the fuck you please."

"No." I argue, "that's *not* what I mean. That misses the spirit of *autonomy."*

We're on two entirely different tracks. I can't get on his; he can't get on mine.

I need to clear a space in this ungodly scene to find myself. *Maybe he's right. Maybe I'm arrogant and uncharitable by refusing to give him the one thing he's asking for. Maybe I'm withholding, adamant, and on a point of pride, refusing to let anyone tell me what to do. Maybe I'm acting superior because of semantics and a different understanding of the word "autonomy." Or is there something else that hits closer to the truth?*

I answer my own question. *The truth is, this is also about integrity. I can't agree to what he's asking, as much as I'd like to, because I already know that I can't follow through.*

"You're asking me *not* to see Charles or talk to him, and that's virtually impossible." I look up at him; he's still standing over me. "What am I supposed to do, turn away when I see him? Pretend I don't see him? That puts me in a double-bind and off-side with myself. I'm sorry, Colin, I can't do that."

"Well, thanks for nothing." He turns abruptly and leaves as suddenly as he appeared.

The bath water has turned tepid. I climb out of the tub and dry myself with a thick oversized towel, my movements as slow and deliberate as those of a sleepwalker. I glance towards the open doorway of his bedroom. The room is totally dark. The curtains closed. The lights snuffed out. The invitation revoked.

I make my way down the stairs to the guest bedroom and climb into bed, finding little comfort in the thought that instead of pinching myself to see if my good fortune is real, like Pieter, the Dutch boy who holds back the sea, I should be using my finger to plug the hole in the dyke.

Alone in the House

In my dream I'm staying with Colin for the night. His house is in an isolated setting. No sooner do we arrive than he begins to leave. I'm startled and distressed and ask him to stay. I want him to connect with me emotionally and physically, yet he refuses. He is self-righteous but does not tell me why he is leaving. As he walks out the door, I call to him through a lower chute, "I think this is unfair of you to leave me like this." Still he leaves.

After he's gone, I lock the doors and pull the curtains shut, fortressing myself in. I see a group of young people outside and feel afraid. Colin may be gone for an indefinite period of time. I don't know whether he'll return. I'm stranded here, alone in the house. Without my car, I have no means of leaving.

September 16, 1998 **Gibsons, British Columbia**

bail \ˈbā(ə)l *vb* to parachute from a damaged boat or airplane; to remove water from a boat by dipping and throwing.

"Bless me, Father, for I have sinned. It has been almost four months ... since I last wrote in my journal."

Silence greets me from the other side of the imaginary, curtained vestibule. The tiny closet of a room remains confessional quiet. I wait for prompting; I know someone is there. Finally I interpret the silence to mean, "Go on. I'm listening."

I address the invisible presence, "I know this requires some explanation."

I hesitate, expecting some response. Receiving none, I continue, reaching simultaneously for absolution and resolution.

"During my first year with Colin, the dreamer within me remained relatively quiet. She didn't have too much to say about what was happening. But after that incident in his bathroom, and the dream that came shortly after (his leaving me unexpectedly and my not knowing when, or if, he'd return), the stuffing's been knocked out of me. And this inner commentator of mine—well, I can't shut her up. She's slammed me with one dream after another, all of them desolate and alarming in a relentlessly dreary way. The only exception is this morning's dream, which falls on what would have been my parents' fifty-sixth wedding anniversary if they were still alive. It changes my emotional outlook somewhat,

shining a ray of sunshine on an otherwise dark landscape. After a week of incessant rain, it looks like there might be a change in the weather.

"Yes, that's right. Metaphorically, as well as literally. With the sudden injection of hope from today's dream, I'm granted a reprieve from this recent psychic hammering and finally have the nerve to reflect upon the summer—as relayed through my dreams. But they've worn me thin.

"My skin has become porous, like a sieve. Like the weather, I'm all water and tears. These past two weeks, I can't stop crying. It's as if a huge backlog of unshed tears, the whole litany of large and small losses, accumulated throughout a lifetime and never sufficiently grieved, is suddenly unleashed. Grief over the loss of my parents, several of my friends, a cousin the same age as I am, and anniversaries of their deaths, which fall around this time of year. Grief, also, over the end of my marriage and other relationships, is spilling out and over me. The rainy season of the year coincides with my pain, pain that I've expressed mainly through words but rarely through tears. The dyke cannot hold back the water any longer.

"Without exception the dreams are cold, clinical and dispassionate, devoid of colour or any feeling of connection. Effectively, they have cut through any illusion of comfort that I may have felt earlier this year, in the spring, either about my relationship with Colin or my career. I can ignore them no longer; they demand attention and broadcast the diagnosis, Something's wrong here!

"In one dream, a man cuts away pieces of flesh (a pound of flesh) from my right arm, apparently to fit some notion of how I should be. I watch passively throughout the procedure.

"In a second dream, I'm in the upper floor of a three-storey house. I'm aware that there's an intruder in the lower level. While the man doesn't threaten or rob me, I also know that

he's messing things up down there. I try to catch the attention of people passing by, but no one sees me. Again, as in the first dream, I am violated but cannot act on my own behalf. The setting is isolated; the house is wooden, gloomy and in disarray.

"In another dream, I'm trapped on the narrow top ledge of a stand-alone wooden wall that rises fifty feet in the air. I'm trying to think my way out of this predicament, thinking that if I can turn around and use the drawer handles on the wall face as footholds, I may be able to get down safely. But when I think through my plan, I realize that it would be sheer suicide. If I put my body weight on the handles, the drawers would fly open and I would drop to my death.

"By this time, Joann is watching me with curiosity. 'I'm waiting to see how you'll get down,' she remarks casually.

"It's late in the afternoon and I don't have all day. My only hope is a helicopter rescue. Someone will have to throw me a lifeline to grab as I leap off the wall. I must convince Joann that I need help immediately.

"In a final dream, I'm undergoing a medical experiment that involves drawing blood from my left hand with a short needle. I've submitted voluntarily to this operation, yet I don't understand what is happening, nor why the needle is not connected to anything like, for instance, a tube for donating blood. An attendant warns me that the after-effects may include anger. I notice a man with his back turned towards me and suddenly, I want to kill him. I wonder, Does this murderous rage qualify as anger? At the end of the dream, my hand is very painful and I'd like someone to take the needle out, but no one comes to attend to me. I feel duped and alarmed."

I pause in recounting my confession. There's no response. I renew my attempts to engage the unseen other.

"So," I ask, "can you understand how these dreams would eat away at my sense of confidence? My sense of well-being? It's as if they've siphoned off my energy."

Still there's no response. I change my tack.

"But that's not to say there haven't been some lovely times over the summer, as well. For instance, the week when Colin and I took Sarah and her friend boating. In many ways, it was wonderful. But, still, there was that unhappy—no—silly incident that put a damper on the trip even before we got underway.

"It was the fourth of July, exactly one year after Colin and I began our relationship. We were ready to leave for a boating trip and there was only one thing that I hadn't done. I hadn't let my one regular counselling client know I'd be gone for a week and I wasn't comfortable leaving without talking to him.

"With Colin and the girls bustling around downstairs, I go upstairs to use the phone in Colin's bedroom. When I put the call through to my client, he's not there. But, in order to protect his privacy, I leave the simplest, even cryptic message that he'll translate to mean, "I won't be able to see you for a week." Nothing more.

"I hang up the phone, satisfied that I've taken care of this last detail when Colin suddenly appears.

"'Who were you talking to?' he asks.

"Panic pounds through my veins. Was I doing something wrong? And if so, what?

"I explain, 'I wanted to leave a message for my client. I hadn't told him I'd be away.'

"'What's his name?' Colin asks.

"I try to maintain an even voice. 'That's a matter of confidentiality,' I say. 'I can't give you his name, nor would it serve any purpose.'

"He responds querulously, 'On our first anniversary and

you're sneaking calls into another man? How is that supposed to make me feel?'

"I try to reason with him, 'You know, this is the first time I've encountered this situation. I'm new at counselling and still feeling my way around. The last time I saw him, I forgot to mention I'd be away. I'm just showing him the same respect you show your own customers. That's all I was doing.'

"He's bringing out the bogeyman's bag again, only this time he's pulling it down over my head. I fight the fear flushing my body.

"'Well,' Colin continues, 'it makes me think there's something between you and him, or else you'd tell me his name.'"

I flail at the constricting bag, trying to throw it off with a breezy comment.

"'Do you know what my middle name means?' I ask. 'What Alice means?'

"He's not biting. I'm talking more to myself than him.

"I answer my own question, 'Alice means the one to trust,' and drop the subject.

"'You'll have to convince me of that,' he snaps back. Then turning abruptly to leave the room, he says, 'Come on, let's see if we can have any sort of a decent day after this. And by the way, thanks for ruining our anniversary.'

"Once again I feel egg on my face—a common occurrence with Colin. Maybe I'm just clueless at these things, or clumsy.

"But whatever it is makes no difference. Without even trying, I've blown the day and the fourth of July, 1998 fizzles like a wet firecracker.

"It's ironic. When I look at the photos of the trip, everything looks so perfectly beautiful: eating dinner with friends on the boat, girls jigging for fish off the dock, girls rowing in a dinghy, girls leaping off a dock into the ocean. There's no hint of the undertow that we're struggling against.

"So the combination of these things, the dreams and this

incident, has left me feeling strangely unsettled. Then, on top of this disquieting mood left over from the summer, at the beginning of September, I'm told that the two courses I'm scheduled to teach at the community school have been cancelled—for lack of sufficient registration.

"I'm devastated. It's as if the whole structure of my life is collapsing. Suddenly, everything has turned slippery and treacherous. Like in my dream, where I'm stranded on the top of a sheer wall, there's nothing left to hold on to.

"Can you understand how discouraged I'd feel?"

My question hangs in the silence.

"And naive, as well, considering how boldly I embarked on my path two years ago, not the least bit fazed by the idea of travelling an unmarked route with brambles blocking the way.

"I'm starting to lose faith, even starting to doubt the process, thinking that it's less a fascinating journey towards self-actualization than it is a dead-end. At times, when I think of how convoluted my life has been, and in particular, my career path, it makes me sick.

"But when I awaken this morning, the rain has started to taper off and I've been given the gift of a dramatically different sort of dream: the image of a magnificent oversized golden egg. Simple, yet powerful, it administers an antidote for the emotional ills I've been suffering. By alluding to the fairy tale, The Golden Egg, it also suggests magic and the presence of spirit.

"Within the image is the power, not only to quell my fears, but also to feed my soul. Symbolically, this dream tells me that something wondrous is incubating within me. It tells me that I can rest assured."

October 12, 1998 **Gibsons, British Columbia**

retch **\'rech** *vb* to eject violently from stomach to mouth; to puke, spew or vomit.

Four weeks ago I thought that my fall season was *in the bag* with work that I love: workshops, courses to teach and contracts to fulfil. Suddenly, it was reduced to a pile of rubble. The structure that I imagined I was building (both inner and outer), imploded under the pressure of unseen forces, leaving me stunned as if hit by a wooden plank. The conflicting factions within me were *at it* again. The recent turn of events disgusted Athena, who flounced out the door, declaring as she left, "I'm out of here." A single piece of the structure remained standing: an upcoming workshop.

My conviction that I'm creating an authentically powerful life, fuelled by the Winter Gardener's intuition, inspiration, creativity and tenacity, buckles under the strain of my following an obscure path. Doubts creep in as nagging questions. *How can I provide for Sarah and myself? How do I know I'm on the right path?*

I also ask the critical questions that I never bothered to ask at the outset of this journey when I was shown my path in a dream. *Where does it lead?* And finally, *How do I keep putting one foot in front of the other with so little encouragement?*

Still, the Winter Gardener prevails. In her wisdom, she

suggests that we sift through the rubble to discover what our dreams have been saying over the past few years.

Considered as a whole, they are connected by a thread of common themes: terrifying ordeals, shifting values, excruciating pain, unusual responses, buried gifts, struggle, and the need for forbearance. My latest dream, *A Steep Hill*, comments on my weariness as I begin the final confronting round of preparation for my *Lives in Transition* workshop.

Looking closely at these dreams, I see that there is congruence between them and the realities of my life; all point unmistakably to a symbolic process called *Initiation*. For reasons I do not understand, I have chosen my own road less travelled—a solitary (often isolating) path that is at odds with the collective conventional route; a path which requires courage, patience, surrender, trust and a willing heart.

In hindsight, I recognize that each dream carried me over a turbulent passage like a bridge over troubled waters, providing the spiritual sustenance, as well as the answers I needed to carry on. The dreams tell me, *Someone is watching. Someone cares.* They tell me, *There is meaning.*

On good days, I remember these things. On bad days, I must push myself to convey a confidence I do not feel as I promote my upcoming workshop to generate registrations. I need to remind myself what Joy Lewis, the American wife of writer C. S. Lewis, tells him as they talk about her imminent death in the movie, *Shadowlands*.When he protests that life is unfair, she counters by explaining that their current happiness is directly related to the pain he will feel after she's gone. As she says, *"That's the deal."*

I paraphrase her words to bolster my fortitude, telling myself, *The struggle now is part of the satisfaction later—when I'm presenting my work. That's the deal.*

Her promise holds true. When I present the workshop, it is as satisfying as the lunch I serve—smoked salmon on bagels (compliments of Colin) and homemade carrot cake. The sparkling energy I enjoy throughout the day and for several days thereafter confirms what I already know. The financial rewards are minimal, and promoting my own work often feels dreadful. *Still, this is where I come alive. This is where I am real. This is why I continue the work of winter gardening.*

But despite this recent success and the feeling that I've returned to firmer ground within myself, what now feels equally as daunting as promoting the workshop is the thought of meeting with Brian to plan Sarah's Christmas holidays. The topic of a schedule for her, a regular one with weeks *on* and *off,* split between Brian's house and mine, has already inured itself in Colin's and my relationship as a source of friction. Colin's response to our lack of a more formal family arrangement is irritation and impatience. Mine is avoidance and fear.

"I don't know why the two of you can't figure out a schedule for her and then be done with it," he repeats his frequent complaint. "It's really not that difficult. Besides, if you had a schedule, Christmas—or any other holiday—wouldn't be a problem. We'd all know what was happening, for a change." He mutters the postscript under his breath.

"It's not that simple," I come back. "To start with, Brian's schedule is all over the place. He rarely knows when he's going to be in town. So trying to be more specific with Sarah would be ridiculous. We'd never be able to follow it.

"But," I continue quietly, "I think the real reason I drag my feet on these arrangements is that I'm afraid—afraid that if we establish a more fixed schedule, I'll end up having Sarah with me even less than I do now. So what would that accomplish?"

He seems to understand and offers a compromise. "Well, at least, get Christmas figured out. That's not asking too much, is it?"

"I've already left Brian a message, asking to see him next week. So it's in the works. I'll get it done," I assure him.

"But you know what," I continue, switching directions suddenly, "what I'd really love to do is to get out of town for a couple days. Maybe fly to Nanaimo this weekend—it's Thanksgiving, you know—and join Joann and Frank on his sailboat." I pause for a second, then explain, "I've just about reached my limit on what I can deal with right now."

Seeking refuge from confrontation and impending conversations, my impulse is to find safety in the contained space of the boat and comfort in Colin's arms. He agrees with my idea. We'll catch a sea plane early Saturday morning.

When we land at the dock in Nanaimo, Frank is waiting to taxi us in a dinghy back to his boat, which is anchored off Newcastle Island. Once on board, Frank prepares his favourite weekend breakfast—cornmeal waffles—and insists that we taste his latest juiced concoction: a blended mix of fruit, vegetables and exotic grasses. Depending on his fare of the day, we might be handed an apple-carrot-ginger-lemon combination (brisk and delicious) or on days like this, be asked to drink a green potion that tastes like fresh-mown lawn.

"My God," Colin exclaims with mock horror, "this is as bad as eating salad for breakfast."

Frank laughs and shuts him up with the comment, "It'll keep you virile."

Romanza, a new CD which Joann has recently discovered, plays in the background. Andrea Bocelli and Sarah Brightman capture the morning's mood with *Per Amore, Vivere, Rapsodia.*

Once breakfast is over and before pulling up anchor, Joann and I clean up the dishes and stow away in locked cupboards and drawers everything that could slide off counter tops and break. Frank disappears up the ladder to check on the wind and decide if we'll motor or sail through Northumberland Channel to Gabriola Island.

Moments later he calls down from the top deck, "Looks like we'll motor today," then adds, "not enough wind."

The ocean. The postcard-perfect fall day and the comfort of people who love me. Clustered together, these elements settle my soul.

The recent doubts plaguing me begin to abate. In this moment there is nothing I need. Sitting quietly on deck, I look out over the water—watching for seals, or better yet, whales—and reflect upon a recent conversation with Colin about tides. I'm particulary curious about those he calls *slack tides*, which occur briefly between ebbing and flooding, when the ocean is relatively still.

The boat rolls on languid waves and my mind tosses around metaphors about tides and life. *What is happening with my career? Is it ebbing, without ever reaching the fullness of high tide? And what about my relationship with Colin?* Despite the calm water, my stomach lurches on this one. *Where are the tides in all of this? Are they in or out? Or is this slack tide, that in-between time of waiting and worrying? And what, if anything, can I do to prepare for the winds of change?*

"Did you see that?" Colin yells suddenly, pointing off the starboard side to the small dark head of a seal. I catch sight of it briefly before it disappears, taking my musings with it into the depths.

We reach our destination, Silva Bay, at the south end of the island, anchor the boat, row the dinghy ashore, and spend the afternoon hiking nearby trails and wandering along a deserted shoreline. After dinner in a local pub—chicken wings, hamburgers and beer—and feeling deliciously content, we row the dinghy back to the boat and play a few hands of Crazy Eights while Bocelli enchants us with one final song, *Il Mare Calmo Della Sera (The Calm Evening Sea).* Lights are off before 9:00.

Colin and I have been relegated to the V-berth which, unlike the oversized bed in his boat, splits into two narrow bunks with a triangular wedge of space between.The arrangement allows only minimal movement and even less intimacy. We lie in the darkness, listening to water slosh against the boat, waiting for something to happen. Our separateness is unfamiliar. This is not what I wanted.

"Hold my hand," I whisper, reaching for Colin across the open expanse. His hand grasps mine.

Finally, I interrupt the silence—speaking slowly and pausing between thoughts in an effort to understand certain feelings that have crept in unexpectedly. "I feel such deep sadness tonight. I don't know why, but it's unlike anything I've felt before."

There's no response from the other bunk. Colin is asleep. I pull my hand away gently as I slide into sleep, descending into the stillness within where l*ogos, soma,* and *psyche* germinate the seeds of things to come.

During the night the ocean has turned ominous. When I awaken Thanksgiving morning, intriguing analogies about tides and life are long forgotten. Suddenly, the weather evokes more concern than quiet reflection. Even before I'm out of bed and dressed, I'm feeling queasy. To his disappointment, I forego Frank's offer of another breakfast drink.

"You didn't like my drink yesterday?" he asks.

"It's not that," I reply honestly, "but just to be on the safe side, I think I'll pass."

He announces his plans for the day. "Well, as soon as everyone is finished eating, I'd like to get going. It's blowing pretty hard. We should be heading home soon."

I'm torn between staying downstairs in the cabin or going up on deck for air, weighing the odds of where I'm less likely to be sick. Ultimately, it makes no difference. By the time I inquire about protocol for dealing with what Frank calls *mal de mer* and reaching out to grab the small paper bag he thrusts at me, I feel waves of nausea rising up in my throat.

Anticipating that this is just the beginning, Frank points to a drawer full of airline bags, then tosses a comment over his shoulder as he turns to leave. "Hey, have a look at this collection of bags," he says proudly. "You've got your pick from any airline you want—JAL, Luftansa, Canadian. Designer bags, all of them."

Satisfied that I have the provisions to fend for myself, Frank and Colin leave me hunkered down below while they return to the deck to hoist the sails and get underway. After dead-flat seas the day before, they finally have conditions that make for "good sailing," six-foot whitecaps, which are typical of this time of the year in the Strait of Georgia, and twenty-five knot winds.

For the next four-and-a-half hours, as the boat heaves its way through dark churning waters towards home, I heave, first of all my breakfast and later, when there's nothing left in my stomach, sheets of yellow bile into a succession of designer air sickness bags.

God only knows what this is about. Maybe I'm throwing

up left-over grief and grievances accumulated over the years. Maybe what started out as seasickness was just an excuse to heave up everything else that needed to go.

Regardless of the reason, it makes for an interesting scene as I pass the bags up through the companionway to either Frank or Colin who, in turn, flings them and their sloppy contents into the ocean.

"Don't worry," Frank teases, knowing that I hate littering, "the bags will break down in the salt water ... sooner or later."

At this moment, I could care less about the environment or anything else. As we sail into Gibsons Harbour, Frank offers a wry assessment of what's been happening. "If you ask my opinion, I'd say this is less about *motion* sickness than *e-motion* sickness."

His comment rings of the truth.

October 18, 1998 **Gibsons, British Columbia**

bat•ter \'ba-tər *vb* to beat with successive blows so as to bruise, shatter, or demolish; to strike heavily and repeatedly.

Sunday morning following our Thanksgiving weekend, I wake up before Colin. We're at his condominium; Sarah is asleep downstairs in the Princess room. Careful not to rouse Colin before I'm ready to engage in the inevitable conversation about Christmas plans, I lie next to him without moving. My mind downloads the story of my meeting with Brian. Detailed, intact, it rewinds back to Thursday and begins to play.

I kiss Sarah goodbye at the door. She rushes off to catch the school bus. I wander back upstairs, slide open the glass patio door, step out onto the deck, and assess the day. The air is sodden, the deck a slippery sheet of dew. In the corner, two withered cherry tomato plants stand in large clay containers, unhappy facsimiles of their former robust selves. Like the pear tree that offers its fruit to the young woman in the story, *The Handless Maiden,* throughout the summer these two plants remained unstintingly generous, offering me their sweetness on a daily basis. But the last few tomatoes to appear on spindly stems now hang withered and yellow, never to ripen into red bursts of flavour.

I look to the weather for seasonal cues as to what to wear. Like me, it's undecided—poised between remaining obstinately dreary for the duration of the day or swinging, with verve, into a radiantly clear fall day. Finally, I settle on a blue skirt and sweater combination from Joann's store, leather boots, which I've recently had re-soled, and a blanket-style wool jacket. To complete my outfit I select the stunning silver jewellery I bought in Mexico, a jade neckpiece and a large agate ring.

When I turn towards my reflection in the mirror, I look garish and ridiculous, overdressed by a mile. But with no alternative in mind (besides, I'm running late), I dash out of the house to meet Brian. An ironic rhyme runs through my mind, *Something old, something new, something borrowed, something blue.*

I arrive at the cafe in disarray. By now the sun is smiling magnanimously on us. I break into a sweat. Like my counterparts, the tomato plants, I'm wilting. Still, I remain true to my poised persona and suffer through the next hour-and-a-half, feeling entirely unglued. I forget to remind myself that I've been in emotional shambles for the past month. After being knocked off my footings by the loss of my fall schedule, I still haven't recovered my equilibrium. By the end of lunch, I've agreed to Brian's plan.

Sarah will spend the first five days of the holidays in Whistler with Colin and me. On Christmas Eve I'll drive her back to Gibsons and her dad's home. Then I'll ... The plan gets hazy here.

I leave the cafe in a daze; drive home on auto-pilot. It's not until later that night when I awaken suddenly, after midnight, that the shock of what I've agreed to sets in.

In one fell swoop, I've discounted myself and my need

to spend equal time with Sarah over the holidays. In one fell swoop, I've discounted Colin and his own plans for the holiday, discounted his desire to be included in our discussions and diminished the gifts he's planned for Sarah and me. I've rendered him invisible. I've relegated Colin and me to second-class status as a family unit, as compared to Brian and Mary who have always assumed certain rights and privileges. I've also wiped Sarah out of the picture by not seeking her opinion on any of this.

I lie awake for the remainder of the night, obsessing about what I've done. Like the miller in the *Handless Maiden* who agrees to the devil's demands to chop off his daughter's hands, I suffer the shame of knowing that I have betrayed everyone.

The minute after Sarah leaves for school in the morning, I call Brian and pour out my feelings.

"Brian, I've been awake all night, fretting about our conversation yesterday ... about our Christmas plans. It makes no sense for me to bring Sarah back to Gibsons on Christmas Eve when you're coming up to Whistler yourself on Boxing Day."

No response. I continue.

"If we could make Boxing Day the turn-around day instead of Christmas Eve, then we'd both be with her on one of the special days. She could be with me and Colin on Christmas Day, and then with you right afterwards, from the twenty-sixth on—through to New Years."

I add logic to the equation. "We wouldn't be cutting Christmas in half, which is how it looks now." And more logic, "That way she'd be with both of us approximately the same number of days." Still, I sound like a wheedling child.

Finally, I make my point, "Would you consider moving the date ahead two days?"

"Jesus, Patricia," he explodes, "when are you going to follow through on your agreements? It's getting so that I can't believe anything you say."

I bite back the desire to protest. *It's his turn to talk.*

The answer is unambiguous. "Damn it, no!"

The Miller can't cajole the devil out of collecting on the bargain.

"I'm sorry you're feeling this way," he sympathizes in a gentler tone. "But the answer is no." *And the matter is closed.*

Colin begins to stir. *I'm not ready for this.* I lean over and whisper, "I'm going to make coffee," then slip out of bed.

I busy myself in the kitchen. Colin walks into the room a few minutes later, pours himself a cup of black coffee and asks, "So what did you and Brian decide?"

"Well," I begin slowly, "I'm going to drive Sarah to Brian's on Christmas Eve."

He's heard enough to understand the gist of what I'm about to say. Picking up the thread of my words, he lays out the proposed scenario, his voice thick with sarcasm.

"Let's see if I've got this right. You're going to drive Sarah down to Gibsons on Christmas Eve, on the busiest day of the year, and on a terrible highway at the best of times, so that she can spend Christmas Day with her father and then drive all the way back up to Whistler with him on Boxing Day? And, of course, you remember what the roads are like at that time of the year. Hell, you hate driving that highway even in the summer, but I guess that doesn't worry you now."

Hearing his twist on the story, I realize that Brian's and my plan is not only ludicrous but downright dangerous.

"And what about *you?*" Colin continues. "By then it will be too late to catch a ferry and drive back to Whistler. So what are you planning to do? Stay over at your house until Christmas morning, when you can get up at 5:30 to catch the first ferry across? Then drive back to Whistler?

"That sounds really nice, you and me spending Christmas in different houses, with you driving up and down a treacherous highway, when the three of us could be spending Christmas together in a beautiful condo. I thought we'd all ski that day. Then I thought I'd make your favourite meal—rack of lamb. I know Sarah loves that, too.

"And tell me this, why do you think I leased the condo for the season, if not for all of us to enjoy? I thought having a place for the winter would be fabulous for you. But I guess it's not that special.

"So, if that's your idea of a good time, well, way to go, Patricia. It's a great plan."

Instinctively, I place my hands over my ears, cowering at the sound of his words, knowing at the same time that he's right.

My words, when I finally utter them, are laced with self-recrimination.

"Well, I've blown it."

"What have you blown, Mommy?" quips Sarah who has appeared suddenly around the corner.

I turn towards her, choosing my words carefully.

"Your dad and I met to figure out Christmas and I agreed that I'd bring you back to Gibsons on Christmas Eve so you could spend Christmas with him and Mary. And then you'd be with him for the rest of the holidays. But now that doesn't seem fair, to you or Colin, or even me."

She comes over and hugs me. "It's OK, Mommy. I don't mind."

I continue, addressing them together, "I'm so sorry that I've messed things up like this. Please understand that I'm not trying to hurt you. I was just doing my best."

My last comment is not only pitiful but also obscures the damage that's been done. Furthermore, it leaves no opportunity to acknowledge that to some degree, we're all cut open and bleeding.

YEAR THREE

November 7, 1998 to December 25, 1998 **Gibsons, British Columbia**

col•lapse \ka-'laps *vb* to cave or fall into external pressure; to break down completely in vital energy or stamina.

I drop the subject of Christmas for awhile, then approach Brian again. He still won't budge. In an attempt to recapture our excitement for the season, Colin and I pick up the remaining pieces of plans and carry on. By this time, we've taken possession of the condominium at Whistler that he has leased for the season with John, a business buddy, and John's wife, Kay. The first weekend the mountain opens, we're there to celebrate the new home and the upcoming ski season. Colin is treating us to dinner at Hy's, my favourite steak house. Finally, I'm going to taste the Surf & Turf fillet (crab meat with hollandaise sauce on prime Alberta beef tenderloin), for which I've salivated since discovering Hy's in Whistler last winter.

We trudge to the restaurant through slushy snow, picking our way through an uneven path. I'm wearing a cashmere sweater, pearls and a long leather skirt, which I protect by hiking up around my knees. To please Colin, I've left my ring at home. Ten minutes later, we step through the heavy wooden doors into the rich setting of the restaurant. My olfactory memory serves me well; the dark-panelled room smells of garlic toast and char-broiled meat.

We order a round of martinis and shortly after, a bottle of red wine. Somewhere between our caesar salads and entrees, the conversation drags. I direct an offhanded comment towards Colin.

"Oh, by the way, last week I saw that young girl you went out with on a blind date. You know, the one who works for the highways department."

Intended in jest, my idle remark backfires. He bristles, interpreting my words as criticism of either his ethics or standards, and levels a charge back at me.

"You have no room to talk. I remember you telling me that you've been with younger men yourself."

The conversation is going nowhere. My attention turns inward. Dropping words into my brain like coins into a fountain and demanding discourse, a voice whispers, *"I am so bored. How can I live like this?"*

A second voice snaps back, *"How can you be bored with this?"* as if gesturing towards the display of wealth all around us.

Within seconds, the present and future are re-arranged. As the woman sitting in the restaurant, I suddenly become less an advocate for my whole being than a conduit through which separate selves speak. I recognize the voices as those of the Winter Gardener and my ego, which is intent on preserving my relationship with Colin.

"What do you want?" my ego asks hotly.

"I want more," the Winter Gardener states simply.

"Like what?" demands the other.

"Like dancing. I want to dance with a man. Do you remember that night with Colin a couple weeks ago? We were listening to music on his wrap-around stereo system.

"The Righteous Brothers were singing Unchained Melody. "Oh, my love, my darling, I've hungered for your touch."

"'Dance with me,' I implored as I grabbed his hand and dragged him onto the hardwood dance floor. This man has his own dance floor and still he refuses to dance with me.

"'Come on,' I coaxed, forcing myself into his arms. He moved with me begrudgingly."

"Are you still mine? I need your love. God speed your love to me."

"Lonely rivers flow to the sea, to the sea, to the open arms of the sea."

"His arms dropped to his sides."

"I'll be coming home, wait for me."

"'Dance with me,' I urged one last time, 'like you make love to me. Like you mean it.'"

"'You spoiled that for me,' he replied bitterly, leaving me alone on the dance floor, 'the way you danced with Charles that night.'"

"'Well, if that's the case,' I retorted, 'then Charles wins again.'"

The Winter Gardener continues, passion heating her words.

"And I want to dance with a man in the larger sense as well. I want to discover that a relationship is not only about sharing a lifestyle, although it might be luxurious, and not only about sex, although it might be deeply satisfying, but also about something more revolutionary—about healing our injuries and growing together into a new ground of being.

"I want to explore the sort of intimacy where it's safe to reveal who we are. I want to see the truth beneath the projections and lies. I want to hear another's pain and not take it personally. I want to burn off the deadening patterns we bring into a relationship. I want to use the fire we set off in each other to set our souls on fire."

Her voice becomes husky, fierce. "I want to give birth to something new. I want to create something sacred."

She pauses before adding a final, quieter note, "And I don't know if I can do this with Colin."

My ego cuts in, revealing the treachery of a turncoat. "You're bored, you say? I'll take care of that."

The Winter Gardener reads my ego's intentions. "I wouldn't go there," she warns. "It'll cut Colin off at the knees."

The inner wrangling stops abruptly. One aspect of myself has wrested control. It prepares to strike.

"Yes," I hear myself agree brightly, picking up on Colin's last comment, "I've dated young men. One in particular. A young East Indian."

I've dropped the bomb; I watch it explode.

John and Kay sit in stunned silence. As Colin's friends, the meaning of my disclosure does not elude them. I have committed a cardinal sin. I have broken a Big Rule. Shortly afterwards, Colin ushers me out of the restaurant. We walk back to the condominium in stony silence.

By the following morning, I've been branded as classless, selfish, and by implication, sullied. Colin hastens to remove me from the scene, reasoning, perhaps, that the shame of what I have done will dissipate more readily if I'm out of sight. I'm told, "We're leaving. Get your things packed." He is out of the door and waiting in his car while I pause briefly to say goodbye to John and Kay and apologize for ruining their evening.

Once Colin and I are back in our respective homes, he insists that we abstain from sex and not see each other for the next two weeks—while he awaits the results from a retest for sexually transmitted diseases.

Retest is the operative word. We have already taken this precaution at the outset of our relationship eighteen months ago when both of us tested negative (and when anything unsavoury that I might have contacted before I knew Colin would have been detected). No doubt tempering his desire to vilify me further, he stops short of asking me to douche with disinfectant.

Throughout the rest of November and into December, we watch our relationship crumble. *"All the King's horses, and all the King's men, could not put him together again."* By the time Brian recants on our Christmas plans, saying to me, "When you're unhappy, everyone is unhappy," and allows Boxing Day to stand as the turn-around day, the damage is done. The two issues, the botched-up Christmas schedule and my indiscreet confession, bond into a toxic glue. Insult has been added to injury.

The struggle now facing Colin and me is to determine whether, or how, we'll celebrate Christmas. Citing Sarah as an excuse (We don't want to disappoint her by cancelling our plans at the last minute.), we patch together plans for a holiday. When Colin suggests that we forget about gifts for each other, I'm immensely relieved. This seems to be a more honest response to the current state of our relationship.

What Colin doesn't give me in the way of affection or gifts, he lavishes on Sarah instead. On Christmas morning he presents her with a clay piggy bank that he has been filling with quarters since he bought it in Mexico twelve years ago. To be opened now, it must be smashed into pieces like a child's birthday pinãta.

Sarah hesitates, uncertain about how to proceed and not wanting to appear too eager to get at the money. But when Colin hands her a hammer, which is the only thing that will accomplish the job, she flies at the creature with abandon. Within seconds, pieces of clay and hundreds of coins fly in every direction. In less than a minute, the pig is reduced to a pile of coloured shards.

December 26, 1998 to December 31, 1998 — **Whistler, British Columbia**

flee \'**flē** *vb* to leave abruptly; to cease or vanish; to run away, seek safety in flight.

Boxing Day, 7:20 in the morning. I'm up early to wash Sarah's clothes and finish packing her belongings before she wakes up, so that we can spend the rest of the day having fun together until she leaves with her father at 4:30. I place the stacks of folded clothing into the zippered compartments of an old ski bag, which she uses when she travels back and forth between our two homes. At the same time, I tuck a note bearing the number of Colin's cell phone and the words, *I Love You*, into the pocket of her new Gap vest. I tuck a second note under the bassinet blanket of the twin dolls that Santa brought her for Christmas. In the solitude of the morning, I dance a fine line between pleasure and pain as I perform my parting rituals.

9:05. Sarah appears. Still in her robe and slippers, she asks, "Can we read *Searching for David's Heart?*" Before I reply, she curls up on the sofa in front of the fire, book in hand, and waits for me. We spend the next hour taking turns reading to each other. When a change of venue is required, we play Crazy Eights and one game of Chinese Checkers at my insistence. By now we've decided to walk into the village.

12:15. We plough through heavy snow, my feet becoming progressively colder and wetter in my leather cowboy boots. Still, my discomfort is minor compared to the joy I feel holding Sarah's ungloved hand in mine as we wander in and out of shops, stopping to try on hats (laughing at how we look), and testing perfumes. The smallest details of the day stand out in crisp relief against a backdrop of love and impending loss. Each scene appears as vivid as a hand-painted Christmas ornament.

3:35. Time has crept steadily towards the turn-around hour. We head back into the streets (She's chilly now with her light ribbed sweater, but not unbearably so.) and turn towards home. She looks at me and says, "I wish I didn't have to go today," not whining, but just making a simple statement.

"I understand, Babe," I reply, refraining from trying to talk her out of her feelings. After a year or two of an informal schedule, an unspoken respect exists between us on this issue. We know the part the other is required to play and are not inclined to *go on* about our own needs.

4:00. We arrive back at the condo; time closes in on us. Sarah invites Kay to a quick game of cards. I watch them playing on the sofa from a vantage point behind them, observing their easy affection for each other and at the same time, wishing that we could dupe the schedule of its demands.

4:12. I slip from the room and head upstairs to the bathroom where I begin to polish my toenails. Red. British Redcoat Red. A curious response to the scene downstairs but, on the other hand, it effectively blocks my impulse to bolt. With my nails wet, I'm forced to remain here. I have no means of escape from the heat of this unnatural moment.

4:35. She's gone.

9:10. I'm in bed, weeping as I have been for the past half-hour. Colin comes upstairs to check on the emotional climate, takes one look at me, and decides that this is not to his liking. Grabbing a bottle of Evian water in one hand and a box of kleenex for his cold in the other, he huffs out of the room, spitting out the words, "It's always about your goddamned husband."

"It's not about *him*," I mutter weakly. "It's about *her*." He doesn't wait to hear me explain, but even if he did, I would have difficulty wrapping my words around the meaning of this whole thing. *How do I explain that this tearing away from Sarah is a physical violation? How do I explain that I must release this pain that is lodged in my body?*

I can't. The best I can do is wail for my daughter.

Four days later, Colin and I are eating dinner in an upscale Italian restaurant with John and Kay and Joann and Frank who have just arrived to spend the next two days with us. We're excited about snowshoeing tomorrow and maybe, like Kay suggests, when we want something a little less active on New Year's Day, we'll bundle up and tour around the countryside in a horse-drawn sleigh. Whatever we do will be wonderful.

A well-dressed man sits at an adjoining table with two young children, a boy, maybe five years old and a girl, a year or two older. As a woman who teaches parenting courses, I'm drawn to their small family grouping. I glance towards their table and feel sudden compassion for all of them: the father whom I assume wanted a gourmet meal and who never stopped to wonder whether this was the best place to take his children, and the children, who are now too tired and hungry to appreciate any of this. Besides, I imagine they'd rather be at home (or even in a hotel room), snuggled in a blanket, watching a Disney video, and eating macaroni and cheese.

The waiter finally arrives with their food; he serves the father and the son, but when he reaches to hand the plate to the girl, it lands on the floor instead. A commotion breaks out: a father's anger, a young girl's tears, spilled food, a broken plate. It's all a mess.

"Maybe there's something I do could to help," I say, as much to myself as anyone. Still, Colin has heard me and censures any idea that I might have of getting up and going over to their table.

"Don't you dare," he snarls. "That man doesn't need you poking into his business. He's feeling bad enough as it is."

His tone turns my stomach. I fight the impuse to strike back or walk out of the restaurant. Instead, I force back my feelings, trying to avoid a scene that will spoil the evening for the others.

But regardless of whether I leave or stay, the incident sours our early New Year's celebration. Shortly afterwards, we divide the bill between the three couples, pay it, gather our coats and step outside. The night air is as frigid as the feeling between Colin and me. For the second time in less than two months, we return to the condominium in stony silence. Colin marches ahead and I lag behind, walking next to Kay to avoid contact with him.

"He's pretty controlling, isn't he?" she remarks matter-of-factly. I hear her words, but I am deaf as to how they relate to me.

11:32. I lie in bed, feigning sleep, imposing wakefulness

and vigilance upon myself. I must prevent my body from falling asleep and sliding across the frozen wasteland of the bed to seek the familiar comfort of my lover. Tears run down my face, drip onto the pillow. Whether Colin is asleep or not, I do not know; we haven't exchanged a word since we left the restaurant.

2:44. *I'm awake again. Or, have I even slept?* At best, I've caught brief snatches of sleep. My mind is too active to rest—unlike my body, which must remain unnaturally still so as not to wake Colin.

2:55. The stage is set for an important dialectic. In these early morning hours, the Winter Gardener summons my ego.

"Something has to change here," she comments quietly.

My ego reacts with blame. "Why do you make such a big deal over everything Colin says and does? Do you really think he's different from other men? And speaking of that, do you think another man would provide better than he does? Aren't you ever satisfied? Don't you see how generous he is?"

The Winter Gardener responds without my ego's fiery indignation. "Of course he's generous," she replies, "but it's not a question of whether I'm satisfied with what he gives me. It's something quite different. I want him to be generous in the way he sees me." Her words become more forceful as she emphasizes the point. "That's what I want from him, not more things.

"Most often, he sees me in the worst possible light. When he raises the issue of my lovers, either former lovers or phantom lovers in the present, I feel like he's exhuming Bluebeard's dead bodies. Our relationship is littered with corpses. And it's all lies. None of these men mean anything to me.

"Despite what you'd like to believe," she finishes, "these accusations hurt me deeply and suck the life out of our relationship. But more importantly, because he doesn't see who I am, I'm left alone in the relationship."

My ego interrupts, its voice flat and nasty, "I wish you'd cut the drama."

The Winter Gardener's response is simple. *"This relationship robs us of dignity. It was meant to be healing, but instead it continues to injure."* The finality in her voice signals the end of the conversation.

6:21. Early morning, New Year's Eve. I'm awake, feeling surprisingly clear-headed after a disjointed night. My mind is resolved to the decision that was reached last night on my way home from the restaurant, but my body does not understand. It protests bitterly that its morning pleasure, the reaching wordlessly for the other while still half asleep and coming together, is denied. Instead, it must accept the most subtle of connections. More energetic than actual, it lies for a fleeting moment along the length of Colin's body—close but not touching, in an unspoken benediction of farewell.

6:28. I climb out of bed, walk over to the closet, pull out my black sports bag, and begin to pack my clothes. Colin stirs under the blankets. "What are you doing?" he asks.

"I'm going home," I reply, continuing to pack.

He's out of bed in a flash. Within a minute, he's grabbing his own clothes and stuffing them into the first bag he finds. Leaving the bedroom, he stops and turns. For a second, his eyes, watery with tears, meet mine.

6:45. He's gone. Shortly after, Joann, Frank and I also leave, driving towards Lions Bay where I will pick up my car from Colin's house on my way to the ferry.

11:00. I huddle in my car on the lower deck of the ferry, stiff with cold and disbelief. A cassette tape with poems by David Whyte plays on the stereo. A dirge, *News of Death*, informs me about the meaning of this sudden loss for which

I have no words. I Play, Rewind, and Play the poem over and over throughout the trip across the ocean. The words, *"He is no longer here, he is no longer here, he is no longer here,"* push against the numbness of my mind to help me comprehend. Like drugs to soften the pain, they allow my tears to come.

"And it was then, when I said, 'He is no longer here,'
that the night put its arm around me
and all the white stars turned bitter with grief."

The Archetypes

In my dream I have just finished presenting a workshop. An older woman approaches me and asks which archetypes I am currently assessing. In response to her question, I return to the story of Psyche and Eros, which I introduced in the workshop as an Initiatory journey. I grasp the same large knife that Psyche used to arm herself (as she prepared to uncover the identity of her husband/lover) and brandish it in the air, replying proudly, "Athena."

The older woman disagrees. "I don't think so," she says. "I think Hestia, Hermes and Aphrodite."

January 24, 1999 to March 26, 1999

Whistler, British Columbia

rout \ˈrau̇t\ *vb* to dig up with the snout; to come up with, uncover; to gouge out; to expel by force.

It's late in the afternoon of Sunday, January 24, 1999 and growing dark as I turn my car onto the Whistler highway. An electronic billboard flashes ominously at the side of the road. *Extreme Winter Conditions Ahead.* My hands grip the wheel in an effort to feel the road below me, which is a sheet of ice covered by a light dusting of snow, making driving doubly treacherous. Tension knots in my shoulders and neck and lodges there for the duration of the trip. Mingled with the nervous tension of maintaining control of my car—as I wrestle it through increasingly heavy drifts of snow—is the unmistakable presence of another sort of tension. Sexual tension.

I'm on my way to the condominium to meet Colin whom I phoned two days ago saying, "I'd like to see you." After an absence of three weeks, and after two-and-a-half hours on the highway, I stand at his front door, jittery from the strain of driving as well as the anticipation of seeing him again. Finally, I knock. A moment lapses before he appears.

"I was in the hot tub," he grins sheepishly, looking down at his curious choice of clothing. A winter jacket that he's grabbed from the front closet is thrown over a dark towel wrapped around his otherwise bare body.

"I didn't know when you'd get here, or I would have waited."

"It's awful out there," I remark, stepping inside the open door. The frigid air enters with me, clinging to my clothing. He moves towards me; I step into his embrace, sliding my arms under his jacket and around his body. My hands are ice against his skin, which still radiates with heat from the hot tub. He grabs one of my hands and leads me into the living room. Together, we pull off my fleece jacket, sweater, leggings and thick socks, and toss them into a heap on the floor. We make love in front of the fire, our bodies expressing the longing for a deeper intimacy, which eludes us when we rely on words.

Over the next few weeks, we resume our relationship. Still, we do not discuss my sudden departure on New Year's Eve nor the meaning of my coming back to him. Yet what remains unspoken could fill volumes. Hovering at the edge of my awareness is the growing realization that I have unconsciously replicated my parents' relationship, not only with Colin, but also with previous relationships. That night at the restaurant, I was forced to confront the truth.

In remaining silent while Colin demeaned me, in forcing my social self to appear composed, in refusing to let myself leave the restaurant, and in glossing over my pain, I had imitated my mother. And in his haste to judge and criticize, in his assuming authority over *what is* and *what is not* acceptable, in his unwillingness to see the spirit of my intention regarding the family, and in his bullying attitude, Colin was acting my father's role. It was my dismay at recognizing these patterns and my refusal to accept the same quality of smoldering bitterness that marked my parents' relationship that drove me away from Colin.

During my three weeks alone, however, I began to understand that I had accomplished nothing by running away. My decision to leave was in reaction to my fears and not in response to a conscious choice. I had gained no insight into the dynamics that were undermining my relationships. By leaving Colin, I simply ensured that any personal work that remained unfinished would resurface and haunt my next relationship. Running away was no longer an option. I needed to get to the root of the issues that continued to mar my relationships the same way that blight thwarts the growth of plants.

My answer appeared in the form of *The Hoffman Quadrinity Process*, a week-long intensive workshop designed to transform the self-defeating habits that dominate peoples' lives.

March 19, 1999 to March 26, 1999 **Langley, British Columbia**

I arrive at Edenvale at the requested time. The name is deceptive, given what I know about the boot-camp nature of the process. I carry my bag up to the room that I will share with three other women, drop it onto the only unclaimed bed, and report to the opening session. The ground rules are straightforward. No sex, no music, no magazines, no books, strict adherence to schedules, no cross-talking during sessions, and often, no talking at breaks. In other words, nothing that would distract us from the task of looking inward.

Each exercise is designed to bring to the surface the negative love messages that have run through successive generations of families. Throughout the week we follow guided imagery exercises, play ostensibly childish games, and write the negative love messages that we heard as children on large sheets of paper, placing them on pillows in front of us and beating them to shreds with yellow whiffleball bats. We also write brutally honest letters to our parents, regardless of whether they are dead or alive.

Finally, we write letters of forgiveness to our parents as we begin to understand their own pain from a more compassionate perspective. In one writing exercise and in one seemingly inconsequential story about my father, I explore an incident that I suspect contains certain elements that are common to all my relationships with men. I find my voice as a young girl in the story called *Dashed* which I read to the group.

I'm with my cousins and my sister. We're double cousins and we go most places together. We're 5, 6, 6, and 7. I'm one of the six-year-olds. We're with my dad in his new car that he just got yesterday and he's really happy. Jane and I are in the front seat with him. It's like a birthday party, everyone having fun together.

Then something happens. My dad's really mad and there's a loud popping sound in my head. It's something about the car, something about the dashboard. It's a new padded kind, but now it's got a hole bitten into it.

How did it happen? The hole ... how did it get there?

I don't know, but he says I did it. Now the popping sounds come at me.

"Why did you do it?" he keeps yelling.

But I say, "I didn't do it!" and he keeps yelling, "Yes, you did!"

And I start to cry like never before and I can't stop, and the yelling won't stop either. I can't get him to believe me, no matter what.

Where is my Mom? Why is she not here, because she's always here. But she's not here now, so I can't make her believe me either.

I cry for a really long time. Then I go away somewhere and I'm not in my house anymore. I'm in a black swirly place and I get sucked into a big hole that has no bottom. I feel dizzy and I'm still crying. The feeling of falling makes me want to throw up. I know that I'm all alone forever. No one can hear me cry, no one can see me, and I think this is dying.

When I come out of the black swirly place, I don't know anymore if I bit the dashboard, or not. I'm all mixed up.

I feel sick all over again and there's a cold feeling coming from my dad. He's gone away somewhere even though he's still here and I can't reach him. So he must know that I did something very bad.

We don't talk about the car anymore and I don't know what to do. I'm not in the black swirly place but still, it's like I'm waiting for something to happen so I can understand. Then it will all go away. But that doesn't happen either.

And I start to think. If I did this really bad thing—the bite—then maybe I can make him forget about it. Maybe, if I try really hard to be good, I'll feel warm coming from him again, like he believes me.

So I try really hard. But I'm not doing it right, because if I was he'd believe me.

Telling this story releases impacted pain. Afterwards, I feel a sense of lightness and well-being. By the end of the week and knowing the true cost of living out these family patterns (in terms of pain and loss), I am sufficiently sobered to never allow them to raise hell with my life again. When

I lift my whifflebat to pummel the paper messages on the pillow, the words no longer remain in my unconscious mind as inchoate ideas. I call them by name as I lunge at them with the fury of a wild boar, dragging them out of hiding as if they were autonomous entities within my psyche, each with its own compelling, vicious power.

"Shame, Blame, Withholding Praise, Suffering In Silence, Unresolved Issues, Vindictiveness, Repressed Sexuality, Emotionally Remote, Rigid Beauty, Stingy With Affection, Don't Think Too Much, Don't Feel Too Much, Don't Rock The Boat, Deny Your Pleasure, Resentment, Lies, Collusion, Look-Good-Feel-Bad Relationships."

The other participants finish beating. I swipe at my pillow one last time. A howl rips through the silence in the room as my adult self connects with the rage-grief that the younger girl could not express. **"I Don't Need Your Fucking Lies. I'm Not To Blame. I've Done Nothing Wrong."**

April 3, 1999 **Whistler, British Columbia**

staunch **\'stȯnch** *vb* to allay, extinguish; to stop or check the flow of blood from a wound.

Easter Saturday morning. 8:10 and Brian has arrived to pick up Sarah. He's anxious to get going; he and Sarah are skiing today, as are Colin and I. Colin appears briefly to say hello to Brian and leaves the room without joining in the flurry of activity as we collect Sarah's belongings and stuff them into her bag. I take one final look around the room and zip up the bag, passing it to Brian who throws it over his shoulder and moves towards the door. Sarah cradles a plush brown rabbit with pink satin-lined ears whom we've christened Teddy Hare, a gift from Colin and also her prize from yesterday's treasure hunt. The hunt, a family tradition that we've held each Easter since Sarah was three years old, requires that she decipher cryptic clues and travel further afield each year that we stage the event. Yesterday, after methodically working her way around the Whistler neighbourhood, she returns to the front door where she discovers her treasure, protected in a plastic bag and buried in a five-foot snowdrift.

I stand in the open doorway, watching Brian and Sarah walk away. My throat aches; pain shoots into my ears. Instinctively, my hand reaches up to wrap around my throat in a gesture of self-comfort. I force back the familiar feelings of loss that are triggered when Sarah leaves and call out after them, "Love you," and a second later, "bye." My words float on the frozen air like softened crystals. I blow a kiss and they're gone.

But knowing that Colin is waiting for me, I hustle back inside, dash upstairs, brush my teeth, pull on my ski suit, stuff a twenty-dollar bill and a credit card into my pocket, grab my gloves and goggles, and report downstairs in less than ten minutes.

"I'm ready," I announce.

"Great. Are you sure you've got everything?" he asks.

"Yup," I reply.

He picks up his backpack and turns to go. We're out of the house and standing in the lift line-up by 8:45. We've swapped skis. I'm using Colin's Rossignols to see if I like the new shaped skis before buying myself a pair. Colin is relegated to my ten-year-old pink Blizzards stamped with the words, *Patricia Nattrass, Calgary.*

I fail to notice the irony of the switch until later in the morning when we're riding on the chair lift. I look over and see my skis. Only then do I clue into what must feel like a double indignity to Colin: the blatant reference to my husband and the questionable condition of my skis.

He catches my glance. "Don't you think it's time you retired these babies?" he asks quizzically.

"That's what I'm trying to do," I snap back, "but I doubt that I'll be buying shaped skis. I hate these skis. I've never fallen this much. I keep catching these damned edges."

He lets me natter on, but offers neither sympathy nor advice. Instead, we sit next to each other like perfect strangers on the swinging seat of the chair lift, rigid in our red ski suits.

By now, it's 1:30. We haven't eaten since breakfast. I'm discouraged, sore from falling, losing confidence, missing my daughter, and shaky from the lack of food. Suddenly, I begin crying; my tears steam up the lenses of my goggles and soak the thin strips of foam lining the inside. I feel like a fool.

"Please, Colin, can't we just go inside and get some food?" I beg. "I'm really starting to lose it."

We climb off the lift at the Rendezvous Lodge. "Go inside and get some food," he directs. "I'll grab something for myself and wait for you outside."

We head into the lodge, making our way towards different food kiosks. I grab a piece of Hawaiian pizza, a cup of hot chocolate, and carry my tray outside to the deck to wait for Colin. He's nowhere in sight. I choose the most visible picnic table I can find and sit down to wait for him. Two men approach; they ask if they can share my table. There's still lots of room for Colin and I invite them to join me. I'm curious. I can't see Colin although the deck is not particularly crowded. *I wonder where he is?*

Suddenly, I see him. Even across the deck, I know he's furious. Rumpelstiltskin in a red suit, he raises his fist at me in a menacing gesture when I catch his eye, his entire being broadcasting rage.

A voice inside me asks, *"Why is he so angry?"* then concludes, *"I must have done something wrong."*

"Bullshit," a second voice retorts, *"you've done nothing wrong. Let's go over and see what he so worked up about."*

I stand up and walk towards him, taking my time, and doing my best to ignore his outrageous antics. He unleashes his fury once I'm within striking distance.

"Where in hell have you been? Do you think I wanted to wait here for you with my food getting cold and then find you having a party with two men? Why didn't you bother to look for me? I said I'd be outside. When haven't I done what I said I would do?"

Different parts of me react simultaneously. The six-year-old is mad. Mad at being blamed for a simple mistake, mad that she has to explain that she didn't do it on purpose, mad that she's being bawled out, and mad that she's not believed.

An older women is also mad, but in a more reasoned way. *Who does he think he is, treating me like a disobedient child? Why is he blaming me, when I have done nothing wrong?*

Colin is locked into his own tight version of the truth. I have done something unforgivable: I have ignored him, left him high and dry. I have shown that I do not care, or else I would have tried to find him. He takes off like a bullet down the ski hill, leaving me to guess *where* and *when* I will reconnect with him.

Two hours later, I find him at the base of the ski hill, huddled in his vehicle, sullen and silent. We drive back to the condominium and agree to meet in the hot tub to discuss the situation.

He thinks we're discussing. To me, he's railing and blaming. 'Why didn't you even bother to look for me?'

This is insanity—sitting in the steaming tub and feeling stone cold.

Finally, Colin decrees that we've discussed this enough. We climb out of the hot tub, shower and get dressed. I follow his lead. Both of us stake claim to a sofa where it seems that we are *doing time* until the evening's over, with him watching television and me reading.

Perhaps the storm will die down by tomorrow morning, Easter Sunday, when we'll just carry on, pretending that nothing has happened. Perhaps we can ignore the deadening weight of unresolved issues in our relationship. Perhaps by tomorrow morning, our spirits will be lifted, as if by magic, with feelings of love and innocence. Perhaps. Perhaps.

Is this penance I'm doing? I wonder to myself as I lie obediently still on the sofa. I try gentle persuasion with Colin, "Come and sit here with me for a minute." He refuses.

I know. He's made it clear. He needs time out. Still, it would be nice to connect in some small way: a few words, a conciliatory hug, even a wink, or a smile. But he ignores my overtures.

For the next hour and a half, I dutifully cease and desist, refraining from talking and hardly moving. I marvel at my unlikely choice of books, *The Hidden Life of Humans* by Erika Ritter, narrated partly by a human and partly by a dog called Murphy who keeps me company during my isolation on the sofa. His words rise up mysteriously from the page, whispering certain things to me, teasing out a resistant awareness of the similarities of our situations. Murphy speaks with uncanny insight ...

> *I've come to terms with the fact that, in waking life, this is all there is and all there ever will be: these sedate little excursions through the park at the end of a leash. When exactly did that moment come, when I forgot about freedom? And what precisely did I agree to accept instead?*

His words drive close to the truth, but this is not the night to raise the issue. By 9:00, I'm too bored to carry on with this charade any longer. I head upstairs, undress, climb into bed, and compose myself under the covers like a corpse lying in state—not specifically thinking—but thoughts are stirring nonetheless. Alarming, forbidden thoughts brewing inside.

My mind smells danger. *Hush, get rid of those thoughts. They will only lead to trouble.* A sound registers in my head. ***Snap.***

Distinct. Unmistakable. Like a cameraman banging his slate board to notify the crew: Lights, Camera, Action.

Instantly, my thinking clears. An inner voice calls out, *"No, this is not right."* Events unfold without my conscious compliance.

I climb out of bed and pull on my red flannelette nightshirt. Not caring that it is unbuttoned and gaping in the front, I make my way down the stairs towards Colin who is still lying on the sofa. He looks up, dazed; I loom over him, a red raging spectre. Words, fuelled by present and past grievances, burn through my body; rise up into my throat and spill over him.

"I did nothing wrong. I do not need to be treated like a six-year-old child. I am sick to death of you blaming me and never believing me. I am sick to death of you sitting in judgment of me. I am not guilty and I will not be punished." The tirade pins him against the cushions.

Events splice together crudely. I do not see him get up from the sofa and walk into the kitchen, nor do I hear him turn on the tap and pour himself a glass of water. I sit with my back towards him.

Something just happened! What was that sound? My hands fly to my face. *Why is it wet? Why are my hands red?*

I've been hit by his glass.

A woman, who is I, screams; a man, who is he, rages. Walls slammed, objects shattered. *Someone could die tonight.*

A woman flees upstairs. Red on her bare breasts, red dripping through the sloppy nightshirt, red splattering onto her feet, red on the carpet, red on plush white towels. The man follows.

An image of red in the bathroom mirror. Red in her hair, red on her forehead, red in her eyes, red running down her cheeks, red dripping down her nose, onto her chin. Red hands implore him to stop, leaving their imprint on his white t-shirt.

Finally, the bedlam subsides. I'm lying on the bed, sometimes quiet, sometimes wracked with sobs. Colin sits at my side, gently holding a wad of kleenex against my head. From time to time, he throws away the wad and replaces it with a clean one.

My cringing heart opens and trusts again.

April 24, 1999 **Gibsons, British Columbia**

The day my divorce is finalized.

Mismatched Soles

In my dream I'm standing in the outside parking lot of a large commercial complex. I look back towards the massive buildings and parking structures and see that the entire landscape is concrete and barren. I'm trying to exchange the pale green thongs that I purchased for $3.00 because the soles are mismatched. Although they were not expensive and a part of me thinks that bothering to find the correct mate is a waste of time, I'm intent on finding a matched pair. I search the bins located on the edge of the parking lot, trying to get this sorted out. Several women try to help. I feel confused and upset.

Suddenly, I remember that I'm supposed to be going to the airport to catch a flight. The problem is, I don't know where I've parked my car. I believe that it's somewhere behind me, in one of the concrete parkades, but I haven't a clue which one.

By now it is 1:30 in the afternoon; my flight is scheduled to leave at 2:30. In addition to not knowing where my car is, I do not know the way to the airport, how to navigate the busy freeways surrounding the complex, nor what I want to accomplish on this trip. When I tell the women that I'm trying to find my way to the airport, they all agree that it's impossible. I haven't allowed myself enough time. I am hopelessly unprepared and feel trapped and stranded.

The only solution is to wait two hours before I catch another flight. If I take the pressure off myself, remove the arbitrary time constraints that are making me frantic, and refine my plans before I embark, I may be able to find my way. I am relieved that I can take the time I need.

April 27 to August 2, 1999 **Gibsons, British Columbia**

re•coil \'rē-ˌkȯil *vb* to fall back under pressure; to shrink emotionally or physically in fear, disgust or horror.

I've had no communication with Colin other than a brief conversation two days after we drove down from Whistler following the Easter incident at the condominium, when we went our separate ways. He called to ask how I was doing.

How was I doing? I couldn't say. I was still too stunned to make a coherent comment. We groped for words, yet ultimately, they failed us. When I hung up the phone, our relationship remained as unhealed as the gash in my head.

As of three days ago, I am divorced from Brian. This pivotal event forces me to make certain mental adjustments. Without Brian and without Colin (Yesterday, I finally packaged his house key and electric garage opener and dropped them in the mailbox.), I must accept the fact that I am truly alone.

With Colin gone, the last trace of structure in my life is kicked out from under me. The soil where I stand has turned to silt. The winter garden looks desolate; nothing appears to be growing and I have little to show for the two-and-a-half years that I have spent in this liminal passage that I call *Initiation*. I tail-spin into terror. Panic seizes my throat, grasps my brain as it works furiously to understand what is happening in my life.

My reservoir of ideas for creating relationship, livelihood, and income, has run dry. Toxic emotions—despair, shame, self-loathing and weariness—threaten to contaminate the ground of my being.

"Oh, just have a glass of wine," a voice in my head whispers one afternoon while Sarah is at school. *"It'll make you forget about what's worrying you."*

I allow its logic to seduce me and pour myself a glass. When Sarah arrives home, she joins me in the garden room where we talk about her day. Anticipating her arrival, I have placed the glass on the floor next to the sofa where I sit, surreptitiously taking a sip from time to time, then removing it from sight again, placing it back on the floor and hoping that she hasn't noticed how often I'm drinking these days.

I awaken abruptly one night, struggling against a tidal wave of nausea. The room is black. The clock reads 2:47. I grope my way to the bathroom and stare blurry-eyed at myself in the mirror. My eyes are thick and puffy, my face blotchy. *Have I been crying?* I can't remember.

I experience a sense of unreality. Another question follows closely, *What happened last night?* My brain is jumbled. I cannot connect my thoughts.

The questions answer themselves with feelings of abject terror and a dull longing for Colin. Numb with pain, I stumble back to my bed and fall into a fitful sleep.

6:14. I awaken again. The impulse to call Colin slams me like a sheet of cold steel. Stopping myself from reaching for the phone, I wrap my arms around my body as I lie in a tight fetal position. I can't get sucked into the compulsion to reach out for him, and for what? To say, *Hello. I'm missing you?*

As I imagine doing this, I know the idea is pathetic. Yet, this crumb of connection may calm me down. *If I connect with him in this most minimal of ways, will that also allow me to connect with myself? To re-establish the reality of me and, in an even more critical way, to keep myself from floating away entirely?*

When I reluctantly climb out of bed and wander into the living room, I see evidence of the previous night's writing mania. Then I remember sitting at the dining room table, polishing off an entire bottle of fume blanc as I churn out ideas, still daring to imagine a *truly, madly, deeply* satisfying life. Poems, scratched in large ragged handwriting and written on huge sheets of newsprint, appear as testament to my pain in general and my pain in particular for this man, which until now has gone ungrieved.

This is the hole that I've fallen into, one which I never knew existed. The anxiety arrives unannounced, a sinister visitor. I sink and spin, dizzy on a wild circus ride.

Maybe I can spin right out of the orbit of my life. Maybe this seat will snap off from the long metal arm of its mechanical mother and fling me mercifully away—beyond the gravity of the earth that would hold me here. Maybe I can be done with it, once and for all.

During the seven weeks while I've been apart from Colin, a question slumbers at the back of my consciousness, emitting a steady drip of psychic energy. Triggered by a discussion with members of my dream group the day before, the question slides to the forefront of my mind one morning. The moment I awaken, it's there, demanding attention. *Did my relationship with Colin have to end that way?* To my creeping sense of dismay, I suspect that the answer may be *No*.

The question is partially resolved a few days later, the

last Sunday in May, when I present myself at the security gate of the project where he lives and buzz the intercom that connects me to Colin's condominium.

"Will you talk to me?" I ask. My voice floats through the speaking device to the other side of the barrier. I expect him to say, "No."

He answers by buzzing me in. The electronic gates open slowly, swinging wide to allow my car to pass through. I park in front of his garage. Walk to the door and knock. Wait for him to open it. Hear my words, which are not unlike those I imagined uttering one recent distracted morning.

I stand awkwardly in the foyer, wondering what to do next. He steps towards me, takes me in his arms. Shortly afterwards, he leads me quietly by the hand to his upstairs bedroom. We make love, our bodies breaking the tension that has been building in me like a silent scream.

Throughout June and until I leave for a week's sailing trip to the Queen Charlotte Islands with Joann and Frank at the end of the month, I see Colin frequently, yet we keep this fact to ourselves. Our lack of openness about our relationship at this time reflects our uncertainty about a future together. A new question surfaces. *Can I put aside my fears and can Colin put aside his distrust, to create a new relationship?*

The answer to this question remains unclear. Like the mists hanging over the Queen Charlotte Islands in the early morning, the fog in my mind persists. The dreams that I recall from the trip and the subsequent weeks echo the same bleak tone as those from the summer of 1998. They heighten my concern. I struggle to understand the dynamic that drives the crazy dance between Colin and me.

Dreams that I classify under the broad title, *Caged Creatures*, arrive on successive nights during the sailing trip—on the fourth and fifth of July—marking the anniversary of our first weekend together. In the first dream, a snake slithers out of its small metal container and is loose in a room where a christening is about to begin. Despite my loathing of snakes, I must find it, if only to discover what it wants.

In the second dream, a baby makes a dash for freedom by climbing over the bars of its playpen. As it runs towards its caretaker, expecting a warm welcoming embrace, it trips and falls flat on its face, *Squelch!* Hitting the hard ground of reality, it bubbles and spreads like pancake batter. All that remains of the child is its face, which looks up, as if to say, "Uh-oh, now what?"

Questions surface that demand answers. *How have my natural instincts been locked up? What has happened to my intuitive sense of Self? Has my capacity for joy been squelched?*

When I return home from the sailing trip, once again, Colin is angry that I haven't gone directly to see him. That night, a dream that I call *Injected with Heroin*, nails me with information that my conscious mind has been unable to consider.

In the dream I have been with a man in his dark shabby apartment. He injects my left hip with a needle of heroin that he instructs me to leave in. He is dispassionately cold and I am anxious not to anger him. I comply with his demand, feeling isolated and alarmed.

When Joann arrives to rescue me, the man doesn't prevent me from leaving; he is confident that I'll be back for another hit.

Joann and I encounter many obstacles getting me to the hospital for treatment of what I fear is an addiction. This includes trying to find a Yellow Cab, phoning 911 to notify the police of my whereabouts, and calling ahead to the Emergency Room to prepare for my arrival. I spend considerable time writing a picture story about my experience with this man, which explains why I'm running away from him.

We encounter more delays in the admitting process. Joann cuts through the red tape and takes me to my room on the ground floor.

I may be safe, yet my safety feels tenuous. I realize that I have a big job ahead of me, but at least there is hope.

The dream forces me to ask haunting questions. *Is "addiction" the name of our relationship? Is our relationship a "drugged dance?"*

A final dream shortly thereafter, called *Knowing,* requires that I perform daunting physical challenges similar to those in *Outward Bound.*

Task One: I must climb down from a high wooden structure on which I am standing. I feel trapped and vulnerable and will need a helicopter to airlift me to the ground.

Task Two: I must climb a sheer rock face. A man is assisting me on this part of the course. I worry that my clothes—the heavy brown boots and pants—are too cumbersome and potentially dangerous. For safety, I need more streamlined clothes. After serious consideration, I decide, *No, I will not take this risk and jeopardize my life.*

As we prepare to leave the course, the man turns to me and declares warmly, "Patricia." Calling me by name, he *knows* who I am and acknowledges me for saying *No.*

But overall, like those of the previous summer, this series of dreams undermines my sense of security in the relationship. Two questions hound me relentlessly, *Am I in or out of this relationship? What is the right thing to do?*

Two months after I started seeing Colin again, the questions remain unanswered. Whatever shred of hope I may have felt is badly tattered. I long to end the inner turmoil that has been tearing me apart for months.

One afternoon at the end of July—while I'm biking with Colin along a mountain trail—I finally admit that I am powerless to figure this out by myself. I raise my hands in a symbolic gesture of surrender and utter a prayer. *Dear God, I need your help. I cannot do this alone. Please resolve this relationship for the greatest and highest good of all.*

At that moment, I turn the fate of our relationship over to a wisdom greater than my own, trusting that the way will become clear and that events will unfold as they should. Before long, an answer forces itself upon me.

Colin and I are out boating over the long weekend in August. We're moored at a marina on Vancouver Island. It is the middle of the night on our first day out. Colin is asleep; I'm lying next to him in the king-size berth, mentally reliving an incident that happened earlier in the day. Drunk with dread, I spin out of control, unable to ignore the sense that something is very wrong. On the surface, the incident looked innocuous.

Colin had just returned with supplies from the general store at the marina. Noticing that I had used his cell phone (The number I had dialed still appeared on the unit.), he asked suspiciously, "Did you make a phone call?"

"Yes," I replied innocently, not couching my words more carefully. "I was just calling home to check on my messages."

"Who called?" he insisted.

Suddenly, I was scrambling to regain my emotional footing. *What's going on here? Have I done something wrong?*

Reason prevailed. I answered my own question. *No, I've done nothing wrong.*

But the answer did not quell my panic, which continued to reverberate in my being long after the incident. After we hastily pushed it aside; after we sat on the dock watching the sunset; after we shared a split of champagne; after we climbed into bed; after Colin fell asleep.

Fear shoots through my body and another late-night confrontation erupts. I hear two voices: one shrill, the other calm.

My ego fires the opening shot, "For christsake, just cool it. Why do you always react like this, getting yourself all twisted out of shape over nothing?"

The Winter Gardener dodges the missive, staying true to her own line of thinking. "The way that you and Colin never deal with issues can only lead to trouble."

My ego tosses back a retort, "If you ask me, I think it would be wise to stuff that snake back into its cage as soon as you can. And get that baby back behind bars, as well."

The Winter Gardener deflects the charge.

"Maybe you're prepared to deny the dread we're feeling, but this smells like danger to me."

The battle continues. I lie dead-still, terrified that Colin will wake up. And even more terrified that the words screaming inside me will seep into his sleeping mind and inform him—*of what? That I'm terrified of another explosive incident?*

The Winter Gardener finally cuts through the bedlam. Like a prisoner banging against the bars of a cell, refusing to be silenced, she cries out the only question that needs to be asked, "How can I get out of this relationship?"

August 4, 1999 to August 30, 1999 — **Gibsons, British Columbia**

re•claim \re-'klām *vb* to bring land under cultivation, especially after flooding; to recall from wrong or improper conduct; to call back.

Two days later, our boating trip is over. We are back and moored at the marina next to Colin's condominium, cleaning and closing up the boat. My panic has abated somewhat. The luxury of this morning remains vivid in my mind ... waking up early on the boat to a gloriously clear August day and the pleasure of an attentive man bringing me coffee in bed.

I like this and I want this, I hear myself protest. *And I care for this man.*

But the Winter Gardener, resolved to her course of action, sees no need to respond.

I am up on the bridge of the boat wiping down the white leather upholstery and spraying the windows. The familiar smells of VIM and Windex reassure me that we can bring order back to our relationship the same way that I can scrub the boat, and Colin can leave the engines in perfect running order.

My thoughts are interrupted by a song drifting through the stereo speakers. I recognize the voice. It is Sarah Brightman singing, *"Time to Say Goodbye."*

"Shut up, Sarah," I snarl, then yell down to Colin who is working below.

"Would you *please* turn that thing off? I can't stand hearing that song." A moment later, the only sound is the monologue in my mind.

There's too much left unsaid between us. Something's going to give.

When our tasks are finished, we take one last satisfied look at the results of our work and lock up, comforted briefly by the illusion that nothing is amiss. Appearing happy and healthy, we haul our gear back to his home where we are greeted by Colin's mother and a friend who have been staying there. I'm not inclined to linger and visit.

After we pile the boating equipment into the garage, I suggest, "Why don't we go for a quick bike ride? I've got a couple of hours before I have to pick up Sarah."

Assuming he'll agree, I am already grabbing my riding gloves and helmet off a nearby shelf. I jam the helmet roughly on my head and snap the vinyl strap shut—more forcefully than I need to. I hope that the helmet holds back the torrent of words rushing through my mind, which is threatening to spill out uncontrollably.

This is the right time for me to leave the relationship, before the next two boating trips that we've already planned for later in the month. If I don't leave now, it will only become more difficult.

The dream called *Knowing,* which I had shortly after I returned from the Queen Charlotte Islands, has prepared me for this moment. The present reality mirrors the dream. Instinctively, I know that this is the time to say, "No, I cannot continue in this relationship."

Yet the question remains, *How do I exit, with dignity for both of us?*

We've been biking for almost an hour when Colin finally stops. I pull up from the rear and look at him expectantly. Straddling our bikes like modern jousters in full colourful regalia, we stand as if in a face-off, waiting for the gauntlet to drop.

This is it. I know it. But this time, let Colin do the talking.

I've been expecting this moment, one way or another, yet I'm unprepared for his simple irrefutable statement.

"You said things would be different between us," he begins, "but nothing has changed. I still don't feel treated fairly and I'm tired of fighting. I think we should call this quits."

"We could argue about details," I reply, "but I know this isn't about details. And I hear what you're saying. Even though it hasn't been my intention to treat you unfairly, I respect your decision. And I don't blame you." Most of our emotion has already been wrung out.

Tears slide down my cheeks under my sunglasses. "Will you give me a hug?" I ask quietly.

Encumbered by handlebars, wheels and pedals, we turn towards each other for an awkward embrace. This is the best we can manage: the parting physical contact, indirect and impersonal. But his words are sufficiently direct to convey an unambiguous conclusion.

Our relationship is over.

In the days immediately following,I feel like I have just stepped off a circus ride. I'm relieved that it's over and, at the same time, still feel a little dizzy. Above all, I'm immensely grateful that Colin and I have managed to exit our relationship safely and intact, without the drama of my flight from Whistler on New Year's Eve or the danger of the Easter incident.

Five days after Colin and I part, an unlikely event at my home provides a startling metaphor that forces me into deeper reflection. I arrive home about 11:00 in the evening, feeling unsettled after seeing *Eyes Wide Shut* (a sinister movie courting danger and sexuality) with Joann. I unlock the front door and step into the foyer, moving towards the key pad of my security system. The alarm responds to my presence with a scream; I punch in the code and the house becomes quiet.

I stop short; my blood turns cold at the sound of running water.

Is there an intruder in the house? In my shower? I wonder incredulously.

Fear pounds in my brain. I bolt up the stairs and down the hallway to my bedroom and the ensuite bathroom where the sound is coming from. When I hit the doorway to my room, I find myself standing on squishy carpet. My feet are soaked instantly. Slopping across the white carpet to the bathroom, I discover a split toilet tank. Water pours steadily out of a deep porcelain gash. Stunned, I grope for the turn-off valve and twist it shut. My bedroom and bathroom and the entire main floor below, including the hardwood foyer (I failed to notice the buckled boards when I walked into the house.) are flooded. The damage has been wreaked in the four hours that I've been away.

Responding to my late-night call, Joann and Frank arrive to help me evacuate my bedroom and haul my mattress downstairs to the only dry patch of carpeting we can find. For the next few mornings, I lie on my makeshift bed, a castaway on a berber island, listening to the noisy workings of the large commercial fans that the clean-up crew from the insurance company has placed around the house to dry out sodden walls and soaked carpeting.

Life slows down while we wait. I have ample time to

contemplate what this all means, particularly the meaning of water in my relationship with Colin and the message of this sudden deluge.

I realize that water has been a dominant element in our life over the past two years, extending as far away as Maui and back to the west coast of British Columbia, to the rivers we've walked along and explored, to the emerald lakes in the Rocky Mountains of Alberta, to the creek beds where we've waited for the return of spawning salmon. Encompassing the promise of baptism and renewal that was present at the beginning of our relationship, it also refers to the purging and purification associated with the biblical flood.

"Water, water everywhere ..." The overwhelming volume of water that flooded my house becomes a metaphor for feeling bogged down in one messy situation after another. In this case, our relationship, as a container for unexpressed emotion, could not withstand the pressure being exerted upon it.

But for all the water, there was *"not a drop to drink."* In the end, our relationship was too parched to satisfy either of us.

As the clean-up crew moves into the restoration phase, replacing carpet underlay, installing new drywall in areas where it is too damaged to repair, ripping out and replacing the hardwood in the foyer, and painting, I seize the opportunity to do my own deep cleaning.

The down quilts and pillows, which I inherited from Brian, are tossed into the washing machine and returned to like-new freshness. Any psychic residue of either Brian or Colin is washed away at the same time. The remaining suits that Brian failed to take when he left our home are donated to a men's recovery house. Any of my own clothes that I wore during my marriage are delivered to the consignment store. Linen closets are ransacked and pared down to a few essentials. Useless clutter from cupboards is tossed into two green garbage bins that I haul through the house. The ruined bed in the guest room (where both men have slept), is removed and replaced. The guest room is transformed into a verdant sanctuary the colour of spring green.

While the changes in my physical world over the past three weeks have been massive, even more dramatic changes have occurred within the subtle world of my inner being. Something has shifted, which I experience as an absence of the questions that have nagged me incessantly for years: *You call this a life?* And more recently, *What are you doing about your relationship with Colin?*

The constant internal nattering has effectively robbed me of fully appreciating the abundance in my life. But with this recent shift, in the place of questions, which have fomented fear and confusion and drained me of energy, I begin to experience inner calm and a sense of clarity. Whatever created this change remains a mystery, but I am certain that what has occurred is *real*. At last, firmly planted in myself, I let go of my resistance to *what is* and surrender. With my mind quiet, I can finally say, *I am here. This is who I am. This is my life.*

On the morning of August the thirtieth, on what would have been my thirteenth wedding anniversary, I awaken to catch a dream flit across my consciousness. In a snapshot image, a turtle appears. Looking directly at me, she remarks, *"You don't have to rush Rebirth."*

I laugh aloud at the sudden visit by this familiar figure, the Turtle Goddess. Like Hermes' upright phallic columns at the crossroads of a journey, the turtle functions as a marker on an unmarked path. With her comment, she illuminates another layer of meaning, which eluded me when I first encountered her in a dream a year-and-a-half ago. The turtle, as a talisman and symbol for the theme, *Slow But Sure*, has wisdom to share about travelling a journey such as the one called *Initiation*.

Pieces of a puzzle fall into place. I summon the Winter Gardener with the same authority that she summoned me long ago to embark upon an obscure path. Like her counterpart, the goddess Hestia, who upholds a fierce passion for the inner symbolic life, the Winter Gardener responds readily to my call. I begin speaking.

"Not understanding that the path was circuitous ... that it would force me back repeatedly to experience the ordeals of the earlier stages of *Initiation*, or that the process was longer than I imagined ... I accepted each blossom I received along the way as a sign that I had entered *Rebirth*. But I had gotten ahead of myself.

"I now understand that these blossoms were gifts from Spirit to sustain me through difficult passages. My work was less about gathering bouquets than about preparing the soil of my being, by offering up my pain, longing, negative patterns and obsessive thinking to Aphrodite's alchemical processes to be transformed.

"Only then, after the soil has been restored to health, will my soul's garden truly flourish."

Letting the words resonate, I pause before continuing.

"I look over the landscape I have travelled and I am astonished. What I may have lost, I've also gained in a deeper connection to my authentic Self and a greater trust that my soul—through dreams, metaphor and symbol; by urging, imploring and insisting—will lead me to right action."

"Yes," replies the Winter Gardener, "the path to Self is paradoxical. And unless we look closely, we will miss the ingenious design and brilliant patterns."

She smiles, satisfied. "That's the deal."

EPILOGUE

Golden Floor

In my dream I am standing in a bright open room like a gymnasium. What was once a dreary old wooden floor is being replaced with a magnificent honey blonde hardwood. Seeing this new floor fills me with joy. A man is laying down the last few boards.

In my excitement, I begin pedalling my bicycle across the floor towards him. But I do not know that the floor has just been varnished and is still sticky. I wonder how to get out of this predicament without ruining the new floor. The man sees that I'm stuck and quickly comes to my rescue. He picks up my bike, carries it across the floor to the front of the room where it is not sticky, and sets it down. He is unconcerned; the floor has not been damaged.

A friend appears. In her customary quiet way, she affirms the meaning of this new floor. I have a new solid foundation within myself upon which to stand. The numinous quality of this golden floor feeds my soul's sensuous nature and informs me that I am not alone. I am in the presence of a Profound Mystery.

Stage One of Initiation: ***Separation***

Looking Towards Keats Island
embroidery by Patricia Hetherington

Stage Two of Initiation: ***Purification***

The Fire and the Flower Are One
embroidery by Patricia Hetherington
design adapted from Georgia O'Keeffe

Stage Three of Initiation: ***Death***

Dolor y Pasión
embroidery by Patricia Hetherington

Stage Four of Initiation: ***New Knowledge***

The First Night: Integration of the Masculine and Feminine
embroidery by Patricia Hetherington
design adapted from Georgia O'Keeffe

Stage Five of Initiation: ***Rebirth***

Manifestation
embroidery by Patricia Hetherington
design adapted from Georgia O'Keeffe

ACKNOWLEDGEMENTS

Thank You
to the women who contributed their skills at various times throughout this project ...
my friend and editor, Jan DeGrass, for her wry humour and insightful queries; to Audrey Owen for her zany passion for correct usage and for the hilarity we shared; to Denise Guichon for joining me at the starting gate; to Arlene Littler for her beautiful book design and important suggestions; to Susan Beer for helping me at the finish line and for her flare for grammar.
You provided the backbone for this work.

Thank You
to my friends and family who helped me hold this dream ...
Rohanna Smith, Donna Schmirler, Joann Hetherington, Eda Lishman, Wanda Pollock, Barbara Beard, Susan Peters, Zach Franks, Steffie Franks, Nicky Grafton, D'Arcy Davis-Case, Mary Altomare, Brian Nattrass, Sarah Nattrass, Shirley Culbert, Mary Lou Renz, Linda Sonntag, Marion Marshall, Marlene Samper, Sandy Wrightman, Patricia Logie, Pam Roper, Phyllis Robb, Judy Griffin.
You provided the heart for this work.

Thank You
to everyone who asked, "What's happening with your book?"
You reminded me that it was a soul imperative to see it published.

Namaste.

October 2006
Gibsons, British Columbia

Rose Pointe Publishing
1382 Burns Road
Gibsons, British Columbia
Canada V0N 1V1

604 886 9559
www.thewintergardener.ca